ORGAN

Big Band & Swing

Cover photo: Judd Binkert Orchestra, circa 1936

ISBN 0-634-06964-0

HAL•LEONARD®
CORPORATION
7777 W. BLUEMOUND RD. P.O. BOX 13819 MILWAUKEE, WI 53213

Visit Hal Leonard Online at
www.halleonard.com

All or Nothing at All

Electronic Organs

Upper: Flutes (or Tibias) 16′, 8′, 4′
       Trumpet, Oboe
Lower: Flutes 8′, 4′, String 8′, Reed 8′
Pedal: 16′, 8′
Vib./Trem.: On, Fast

Drawbar Organs

Upper: 80 7766 008
Lower: (00) 8076 000
Pedal: 36
Vib./Trem.: On, Fast

Words by Jack Lawrence
Music by Arthur Altman

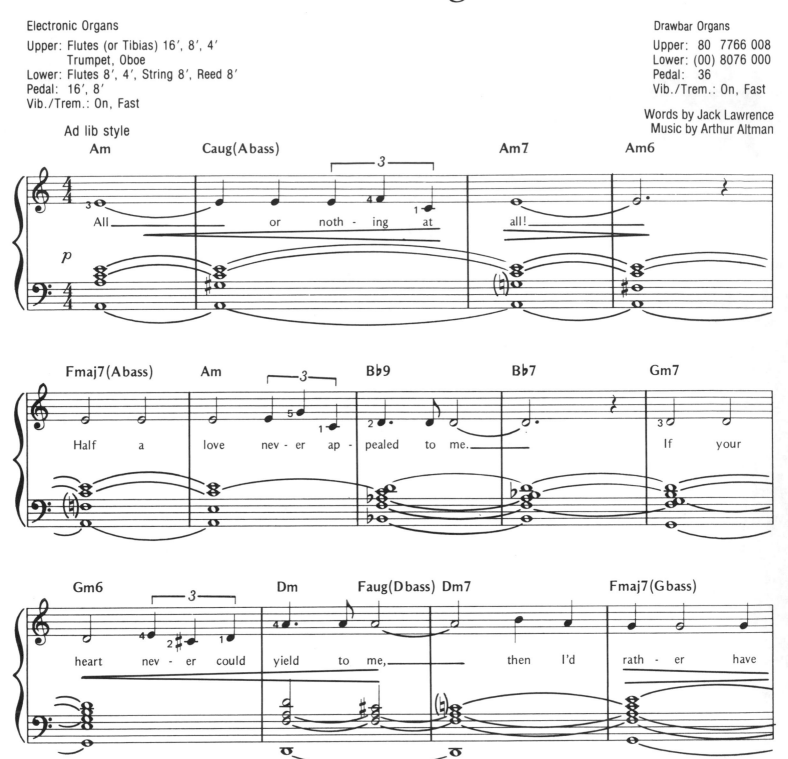

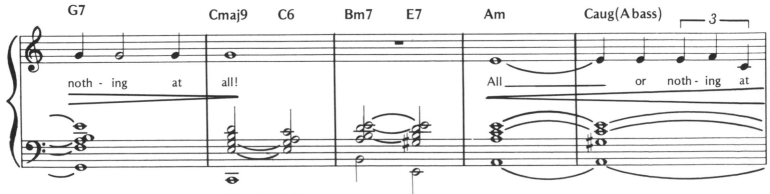

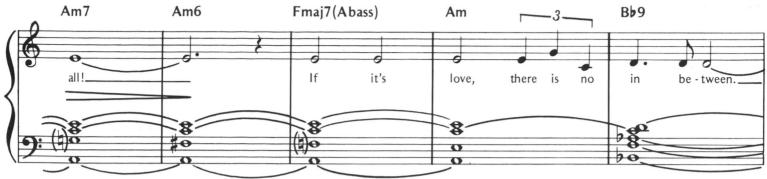

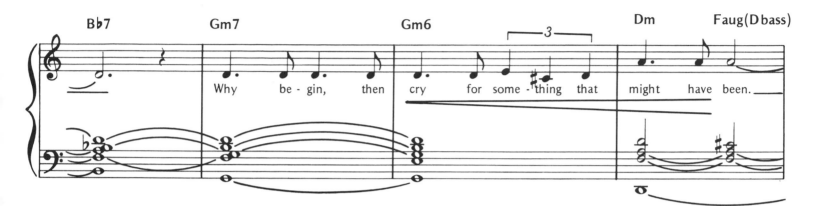

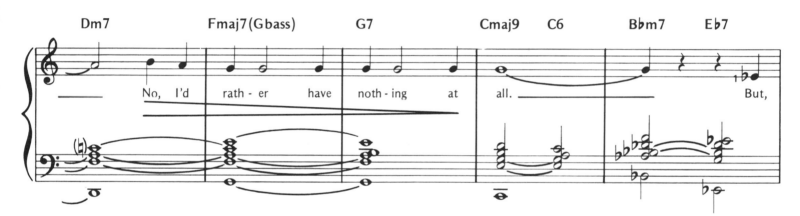

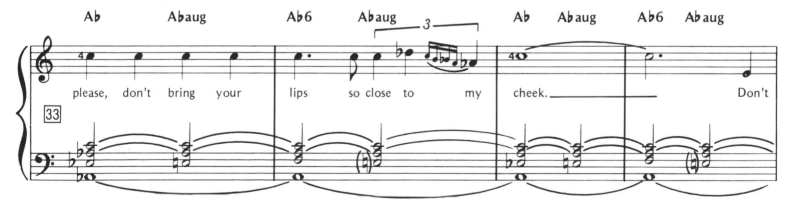

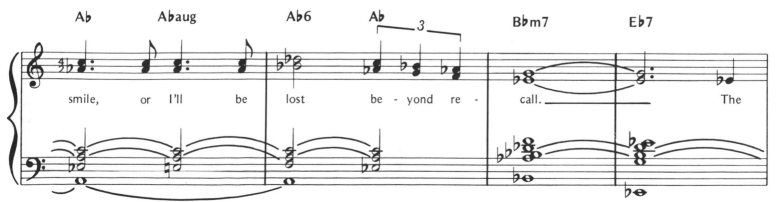

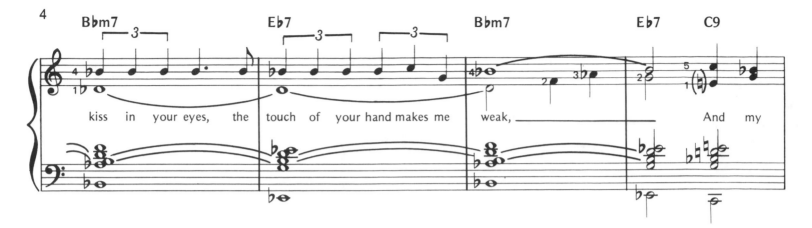

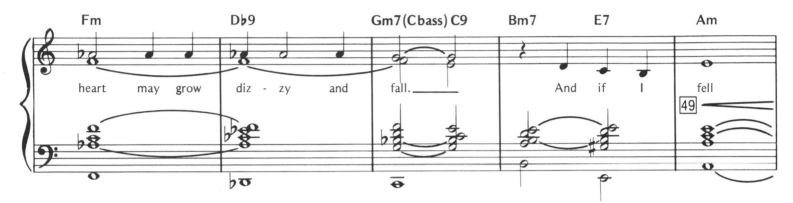

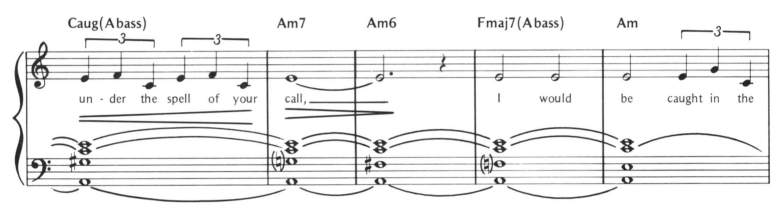

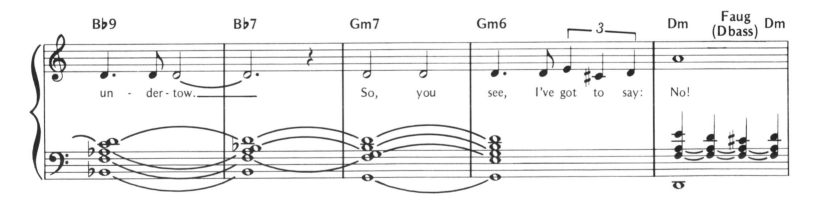

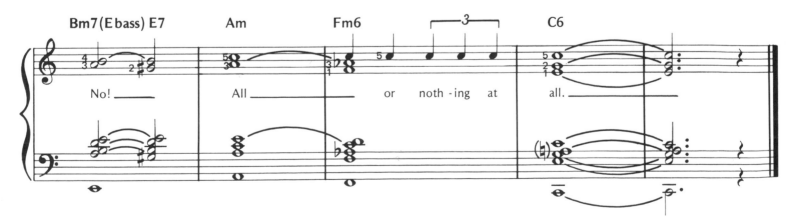

Ballin' the Jack

Electronic Organs
Upper: Flutes (or Tibias) 16', 4',
       Trombone, Trumpet
Lower: Flute 8', Diapason 8', Reed 8'
Pedal: String Bass
Vib./Trem.: On, Fast

Tonebar Organs
Upper: 82 5864 200
Lower: (00) 7103 000
Pedal: String Bass
Vib./Trem.: On, Fast

Words by Jim Burris
Music by Chris Smith

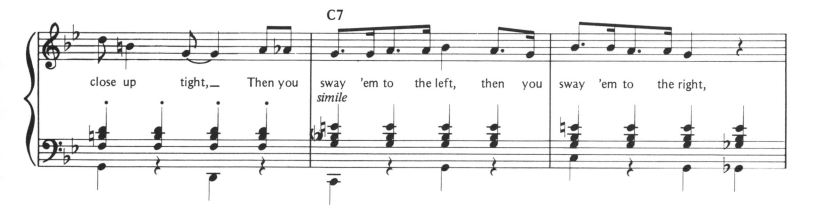

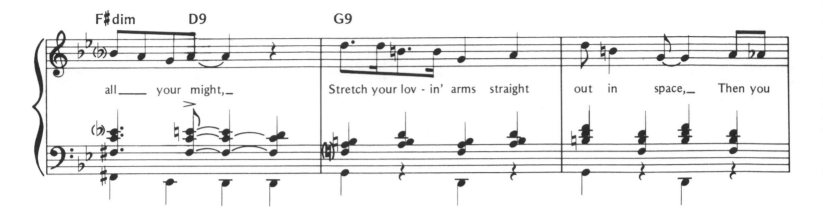

all___ your might,___ Stretch your lov-in' arms straight out in space,___ Then you

do the Ea-gle Rock with such style and grace,___ Swing your foot way 'round then

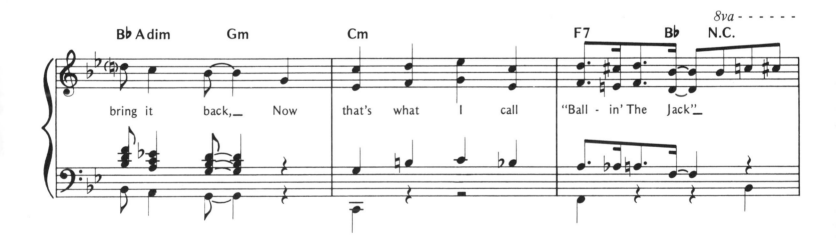

bring it back,___ Now that's what I call "Ball-in' The Jack"___

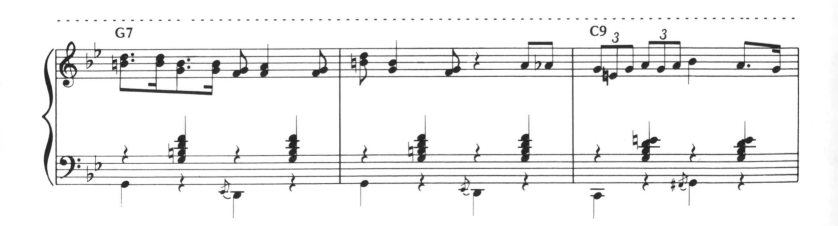

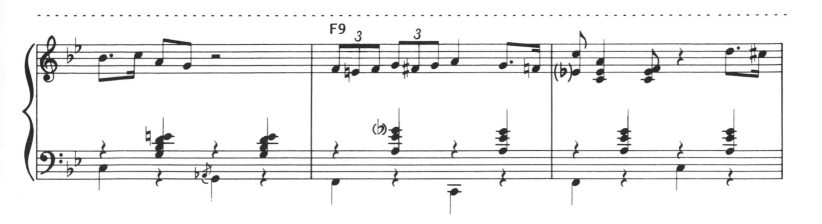

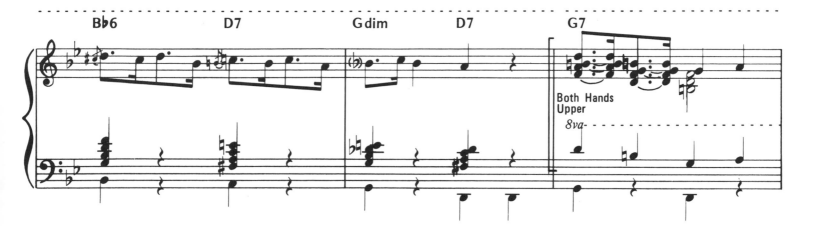

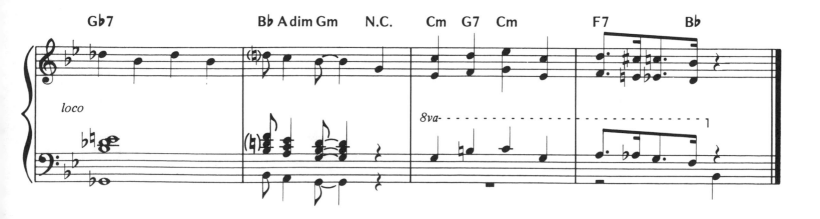

Angry

Electronic Organs
Upper: Flutes (or Tibias) 16′, 4′,
      Trombone, Trumpet
Lower: Flute 8′, Diapason 8′
      Reed 8′
Pedal: 8′
Vib./Trem.: On, Fast

Drawbar Organs
Upper: 82 5864 200
Lower: (00) 7103 000
Pedal: 04
Vib./Trem.: On, Fast

Words by Dudley Mecum
Music by Jules Cassard,
Henry Brunies and Merritt Brunies

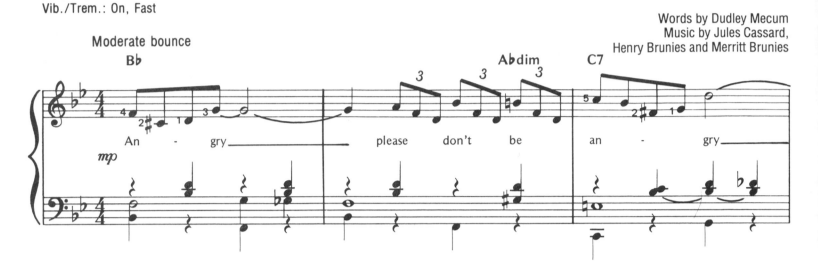

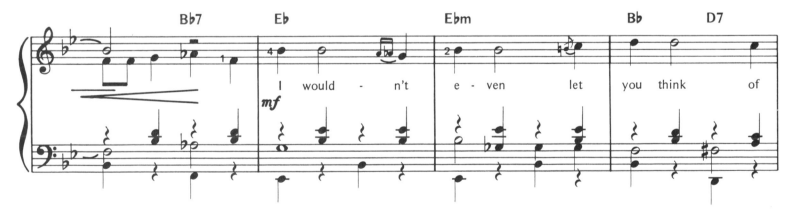

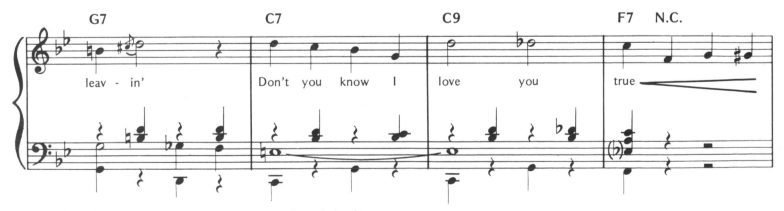

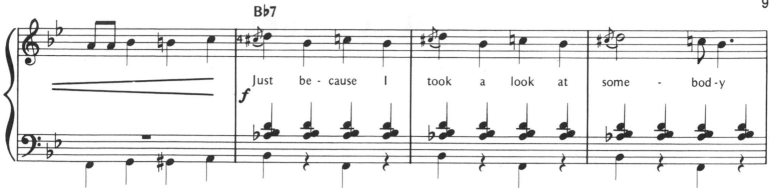

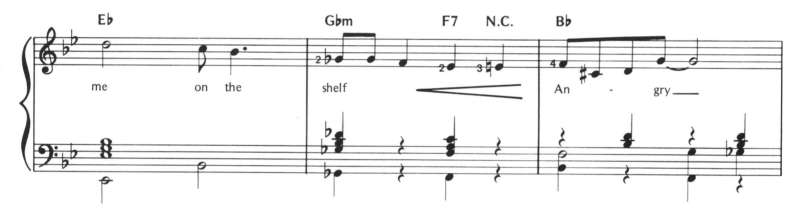

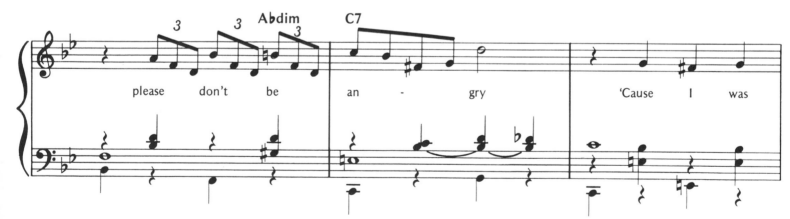

Basin Street Blues

Electronic Organs
Upper: Flutes (or Tibias) 16′, 8′,
    5⅓′, 4′, 2′
Lower: Flute 4′, Diapason 8′
Pedal: String Bass
Vib./Trem.: On, Slow
Rhythm: Swing or Fox Trot

Drawbar Organs
Upper: 85 0000 355
Lower: (00) 8401 007
Pedal: String Bass
Vib./Trem.: On, Slow
Rhythm: Swing or Fox Trot

Words and Music by
Spencer Williams

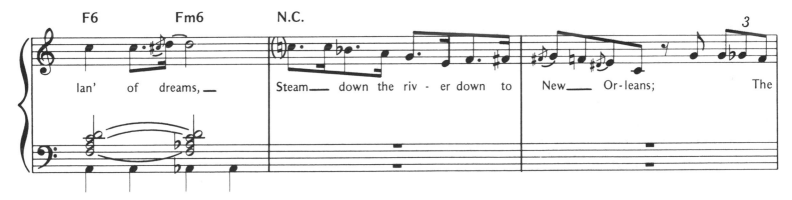

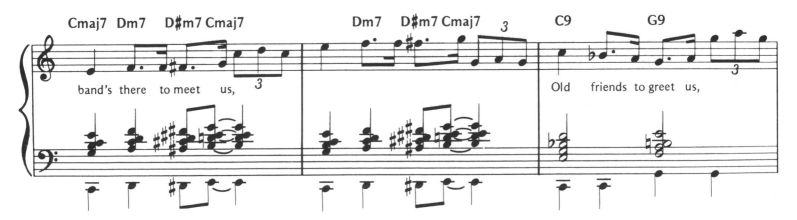

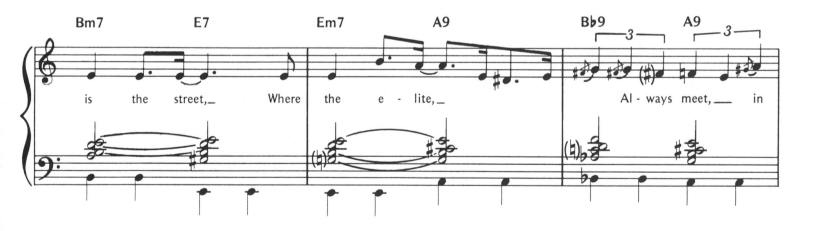

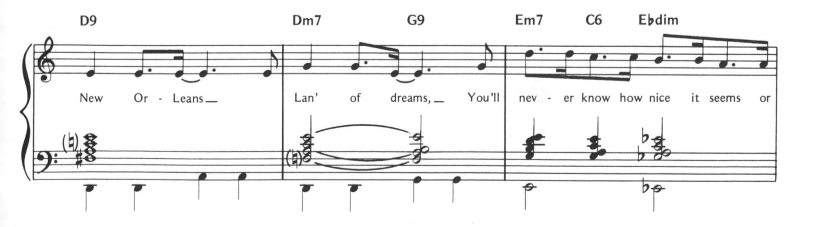

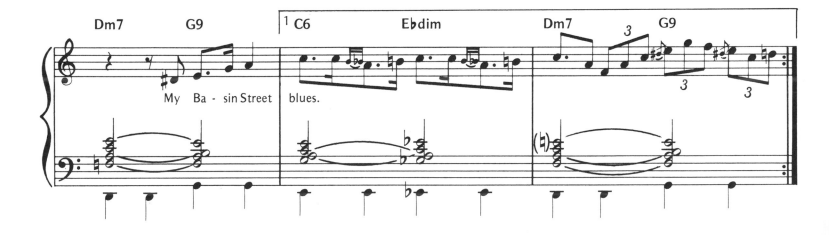

East of the Sun
(And West of the Moon)

Electronic Organs
Upper: Flutes (or Tibias) 16', 4', 2'
Lower: Flutes 8', 4'
Pedal: 8'
Vib./Trem.: On, Fast

Drawbar Organs
Upper: 60 0608 000
Lower: (00) 6500 000
Pedal: 05
Vib./Trem.: On, Fast

Words and Music by
Brooks Bowman

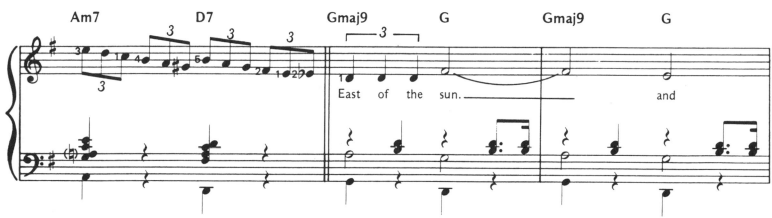

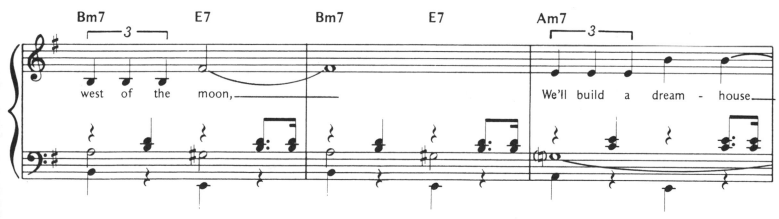

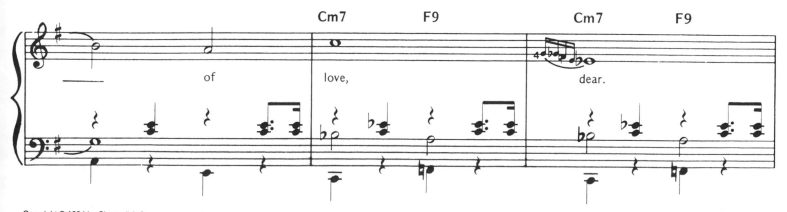

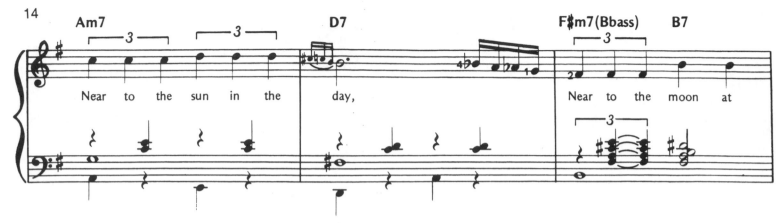

Near to the sun in the day, Near to the moon at

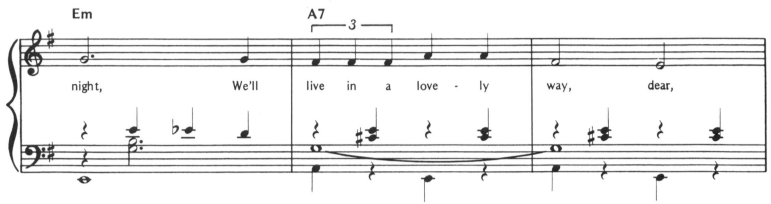

night, We'll live in a love - ly way, dear,

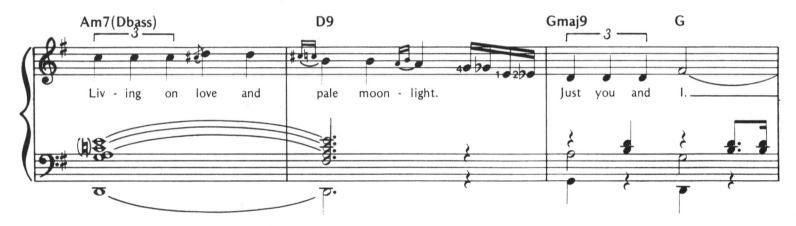

Liv - ing on love and pale moon - light. Just you and I.

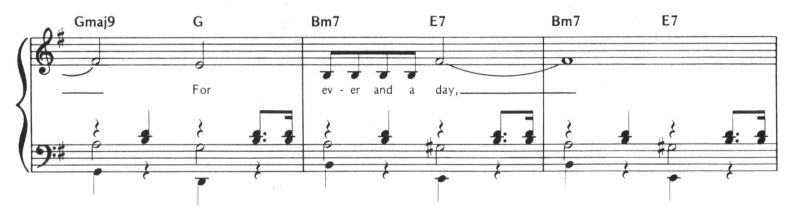

For ev - er and a day,

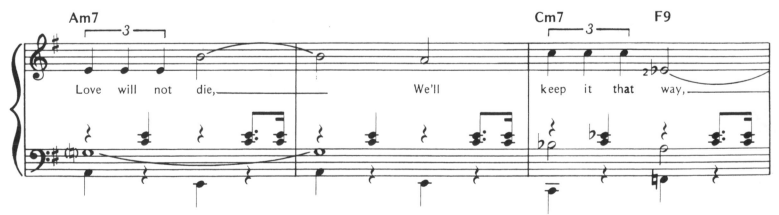

Love will not die, We'll keep it that way,

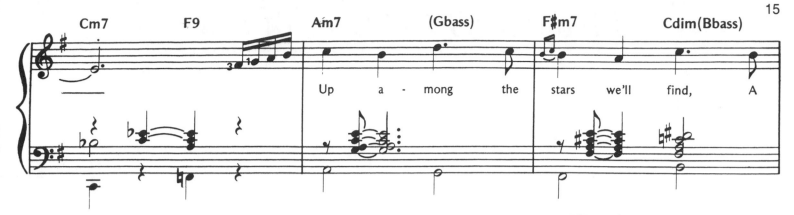

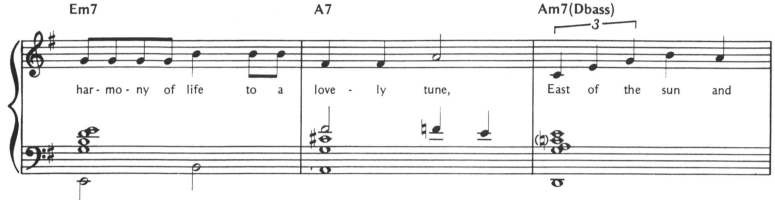

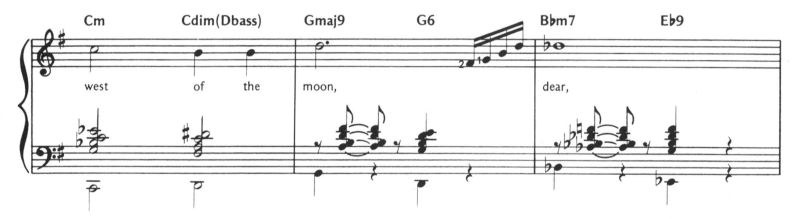

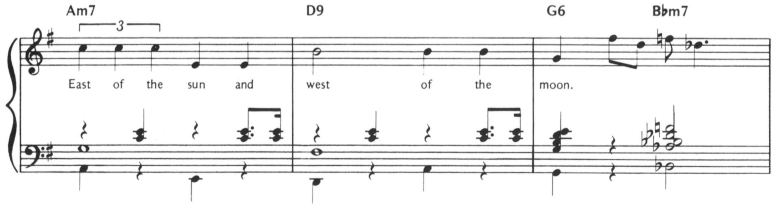

Five Foot Two, Eyes of Blue

(Has Anybody Seen My Girl?)

Electronic Organs
Upper: Banjo Preset
Lower: Flute 8′, String 8′
Pedal: String Bass
Vib./Trem.: On, Fast

Drawbar Organs
Upper: Banjo Preset or
82 6515 004
Lower: (00) 7343 312
Pedal: 23
Vib./Trem.: On, Fast

Words by Joe Young and Sam Lewis
Music by Ray Henderson

Moderately, with strong rhythm

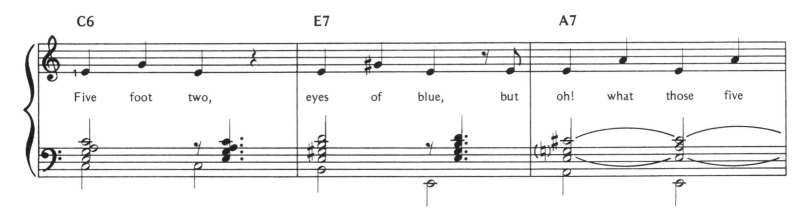

Five foot two, eyes of blue, but oh! what those five

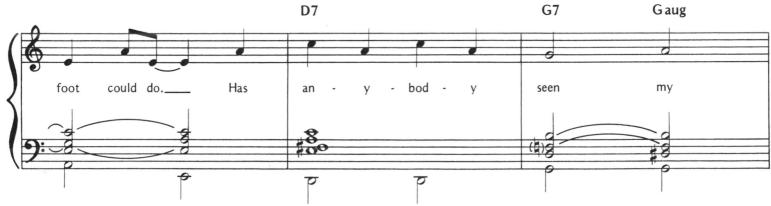

foot could do.___ Has an-y-bod-y seen my

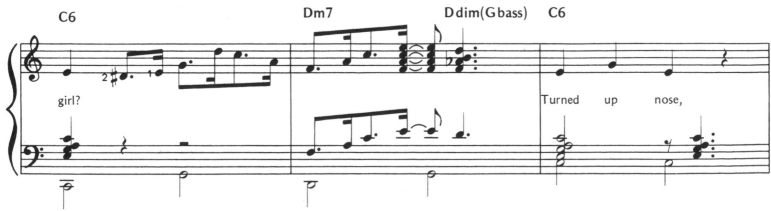

girl? Turned up nose,

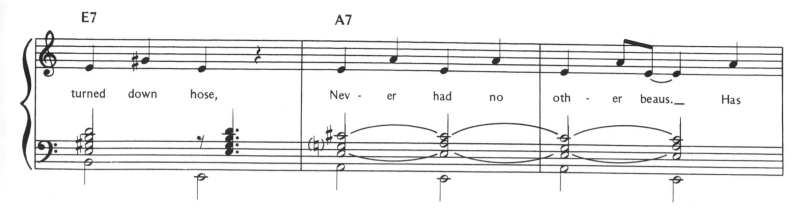

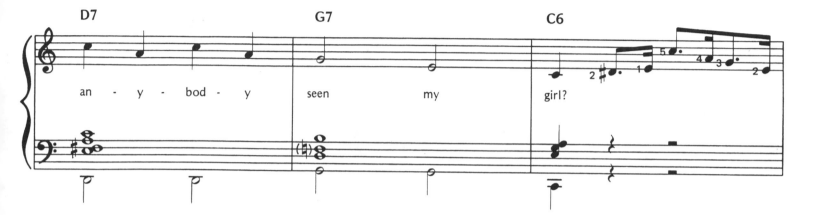

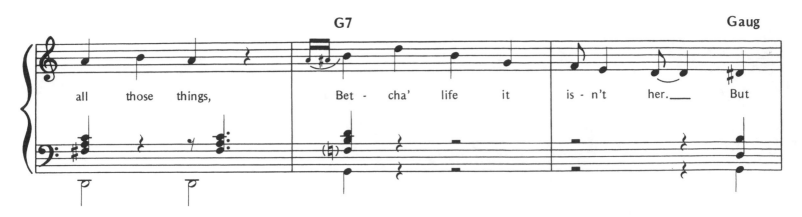

all those things, Bet - cha' life it is - n't her.___ But

could she love, could she woo? Could she, could she,

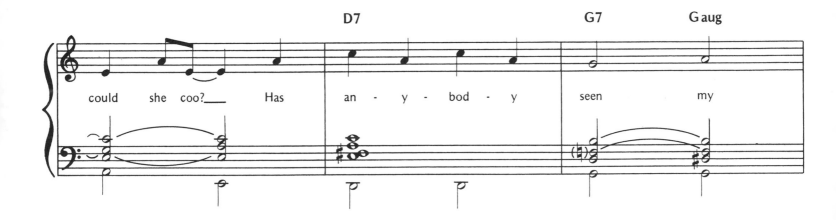

could she coo?___ Has an - y - bod - y seen my

girl?

I'll Remember April

Electronic Organs
Upper: Flutes (or Tibias) 8', 2'
        Reed 4'
Lower: Flutes 8', 4', String 8'
Pedal: 16', 8', Sustain
Vib./Trem.: On, Full

Drawbar Organs
Upper: 00 8006 400
Lower: (00) 7664 431
Pedal: 47, Sustain
Vib./Trem.: On, Full

Words and Music by Pat Johnson,
Don Raye and Gene De Paul

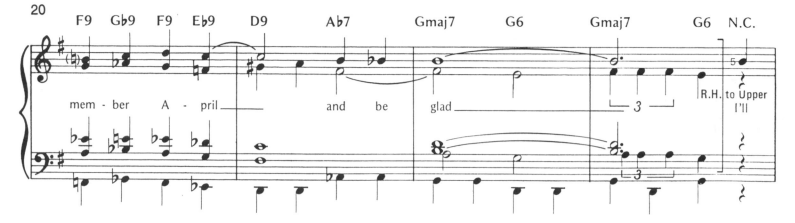

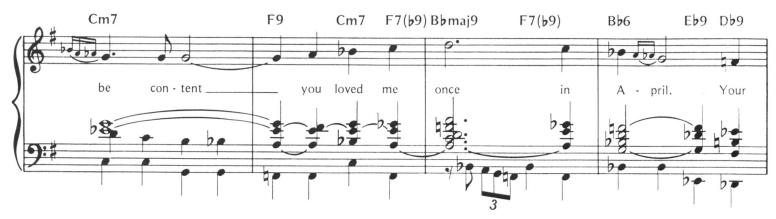

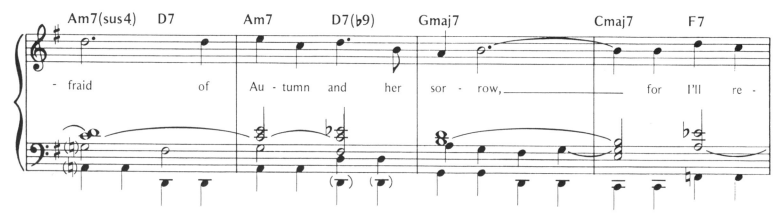

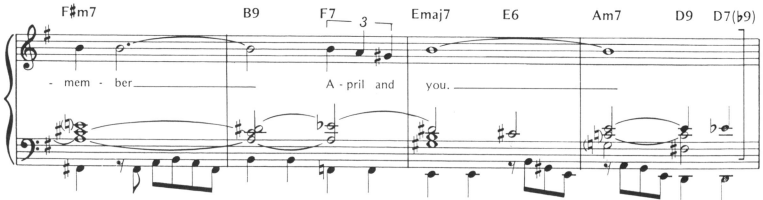

21

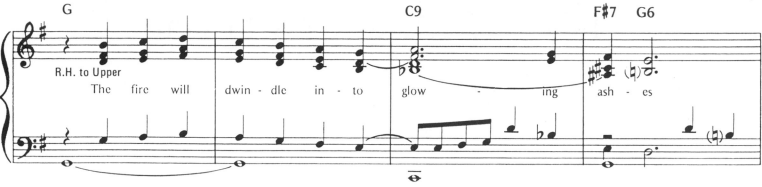

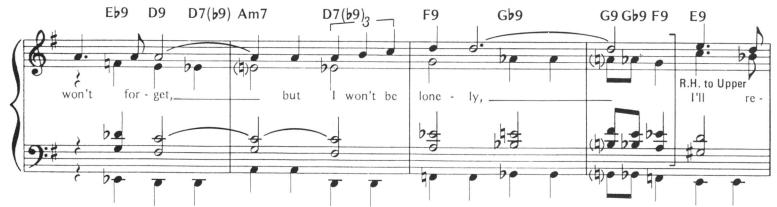

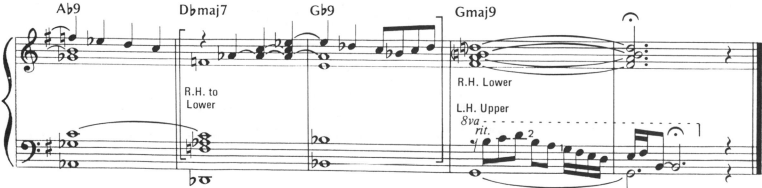

I Can't Get Started with You

from ZIEGFELD FOLLIES

Electronic Organs
Upper: Flutes (or Tibias) 16′, 8′, 5⅓′
Lower: Flute 8′, String 8′
Pedal: 8′, Sustain
Vib./Trem.: Off

Tonebar Organs
Upper: 86 8000 000
Lower: (00) 6540 500
Pedal: 44 String Bass
Vib./Trem.: Off

Words by Ira Gershwin
Music by Vernon Duke

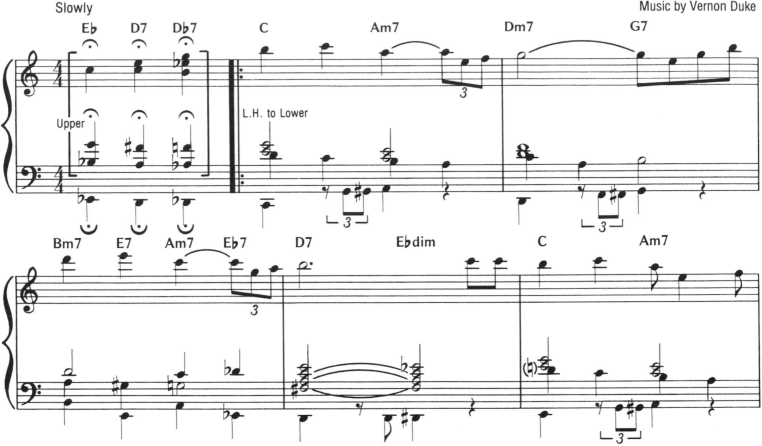

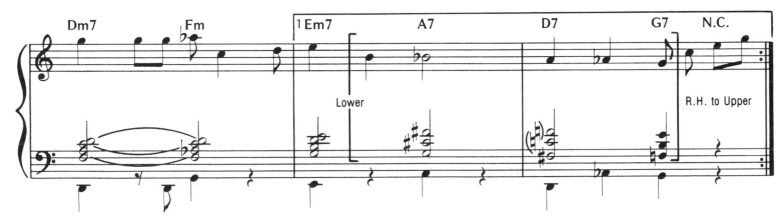

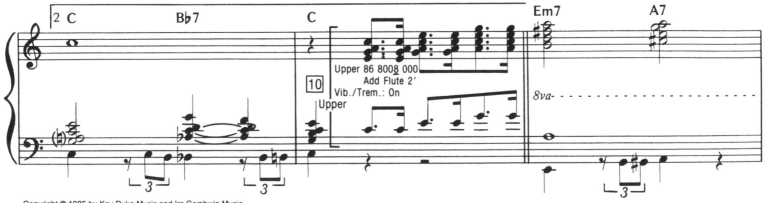

I'm Beginning to See the Light

Electronic Organs
Upper: Flutes 16′, 8′, 2′
Lower: Flute 4′, Diapason 8′, Reed 8′
Pedal: String Bass
Vib./Trem.: On, Fast

Tonebar Organs
Upper: 80 3008 000
Lower: (00) 4203 003
Pedal: String Bass
Vib./Trem.: On, Fast

Words and Music by Don George, Johnny Hodges,
Duke Ellington and Harry James

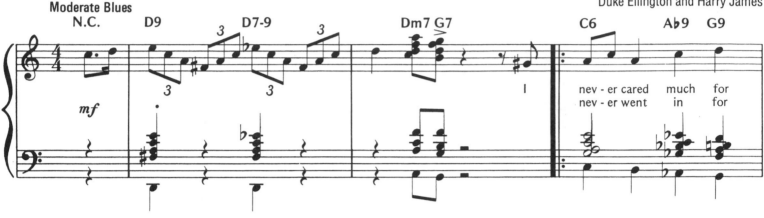

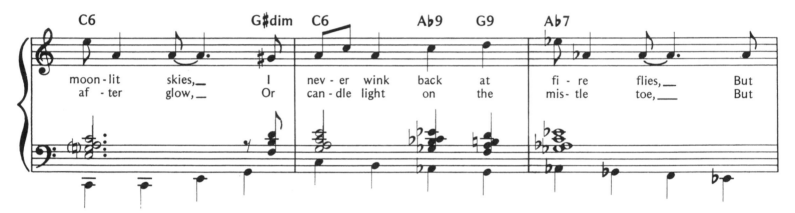

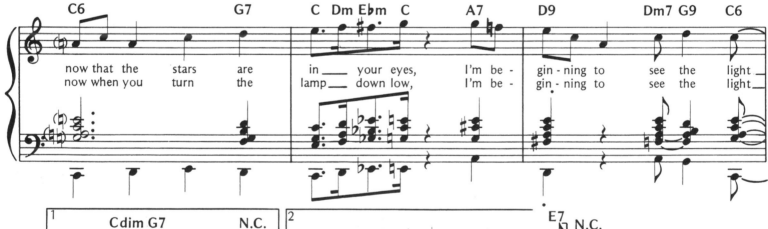

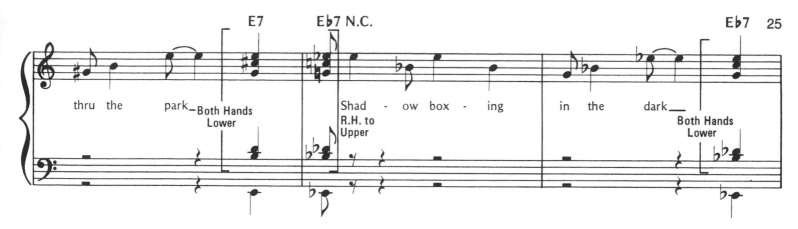

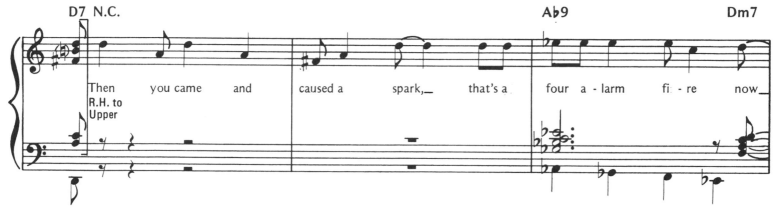

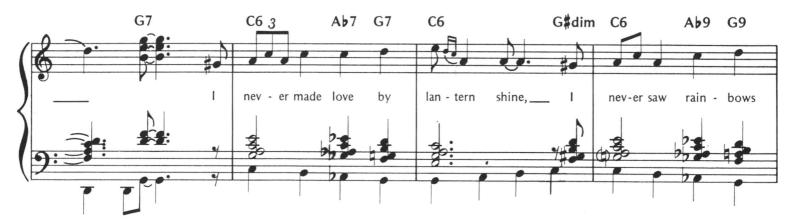

In the Still of the Night

from ROSALIE
from NIGHT AND DAY

Electronic Organs
Upper: Flutes (or Tibias) 16′, 8′, 2′
Lower: Flute 8′, Diapason 8′
String 8′
Pedal: 8′, Sustain
Vib./Trem.: On

Tonebar Organs
Upper: 80 0608 000
Lower: (00) 6504 460
Pedal: 44 String Bass
Vib./Trem.: On

Words and Music by
Cole Porter

Moderate Bossa Nova

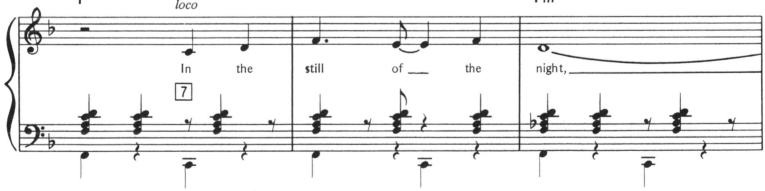

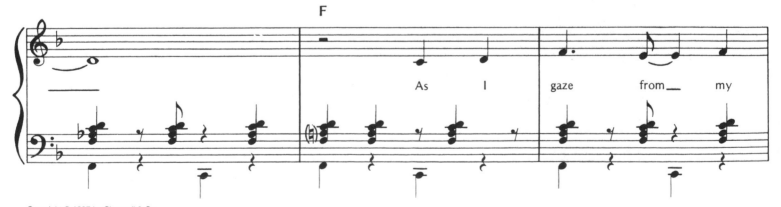

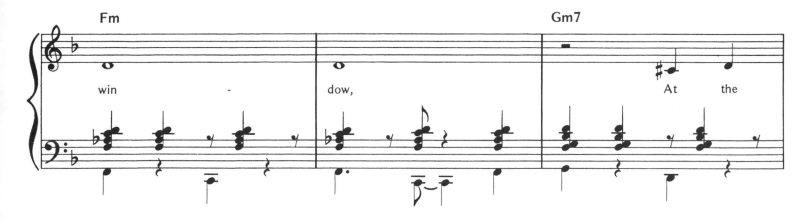

win - dow, At the

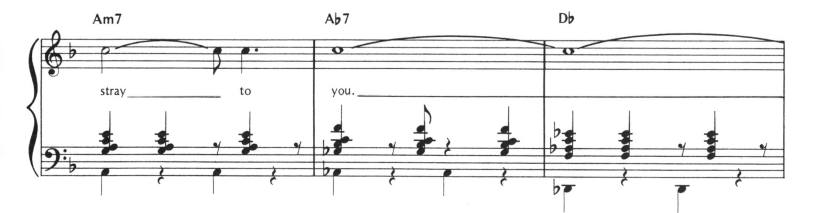

moon in___ it's flight,_____ My thoughts all

stray_____ to you.____

In the still of___ the

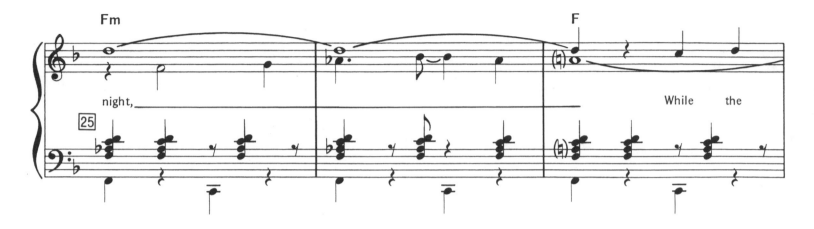

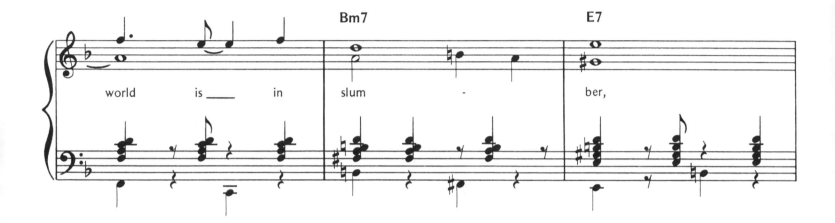

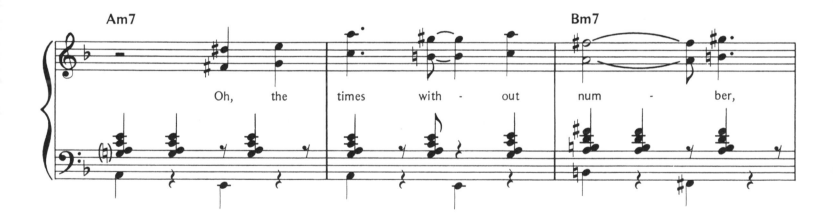

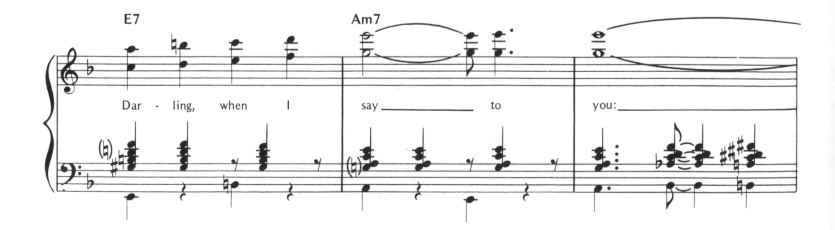

Manhattan

from the Broadway Musical THE GARRICK GAIETIES

Electronic Organs
Upper: Flutes (or Tibias) 16', 8', 5-⅓', 4',
     Add Percuss
Lower: Flutes 8', 4', String 8'
Pedal: 16', 8', or String Bass
Vib./Trem.: On, Fast

Tonebar Organs
Upper: 83 6030 400
     Add Perc
Lower: (00) 6402 003
Pedal: 45
Vib./Trem.: On, Fast

Words by Lorenz Hart
Music by Richard Rodgers

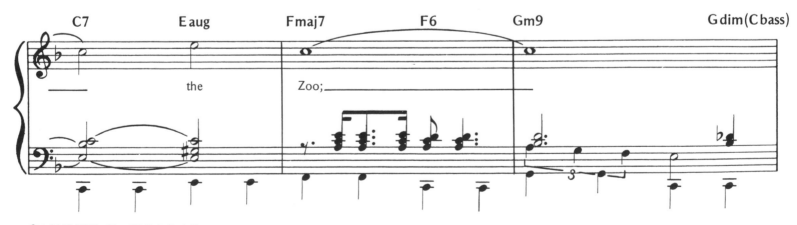

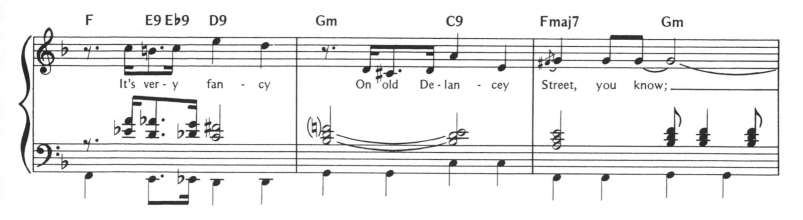

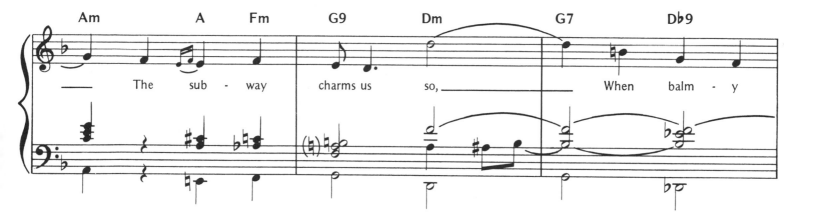

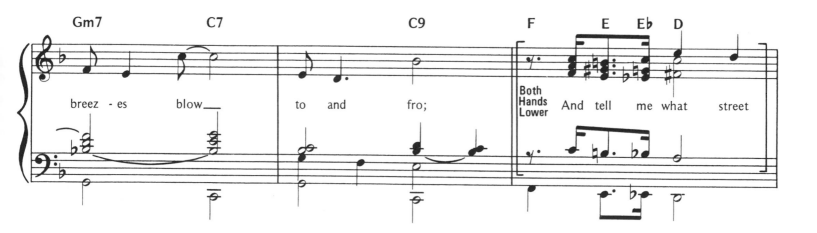

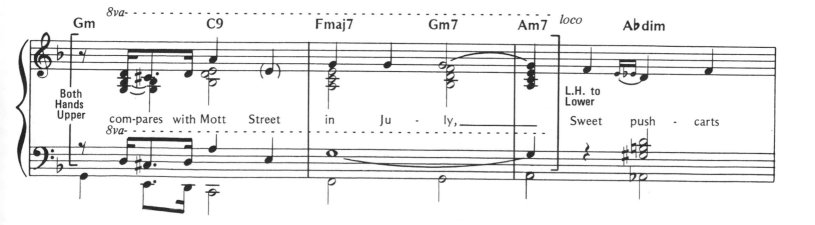

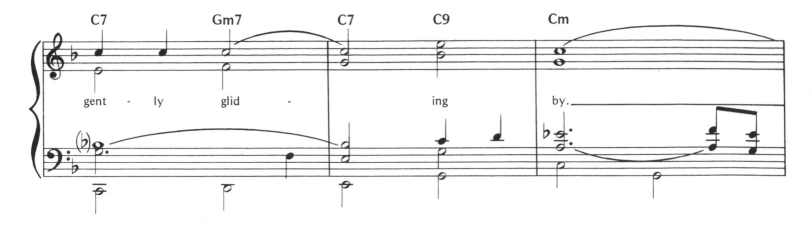

gent - ly glid - ing by.

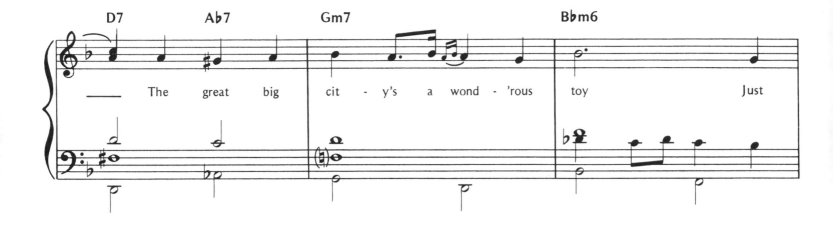

The great big cit - y's a wond - 'rous toy Just

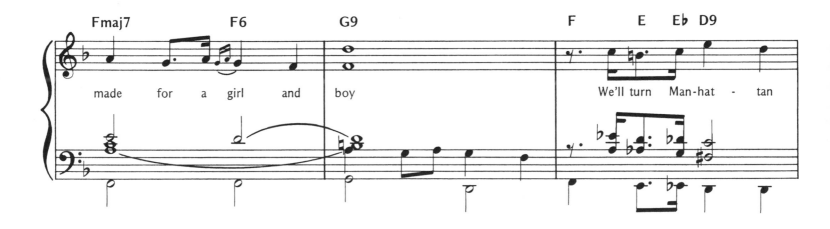

made for a girl and boy We'll turn Man-hat - tan

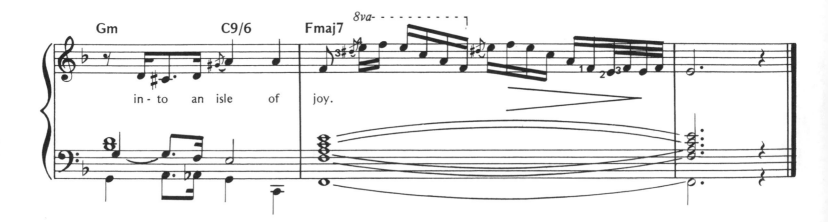

in - to an isle of joy.

Mood Indigo

Electronic Organs
Upper: Flutes (or Tibias) 16′, 8′, 4′,
　　　　Trumpet, Oboe
Lower: Flutes 8′, 4′,
　　　　String 8′, Reed 8′
Pedal: 16′, 8′
Vib./Trem.: On, Fast

Tonebar Organs
Upper: 80 7766 008
Lower: (00) 8076 000
Pedal: 36
Vib./Trem.: On, Fast

Words and Music by Duke Ellington,
Irving Mills and Albany Bigard

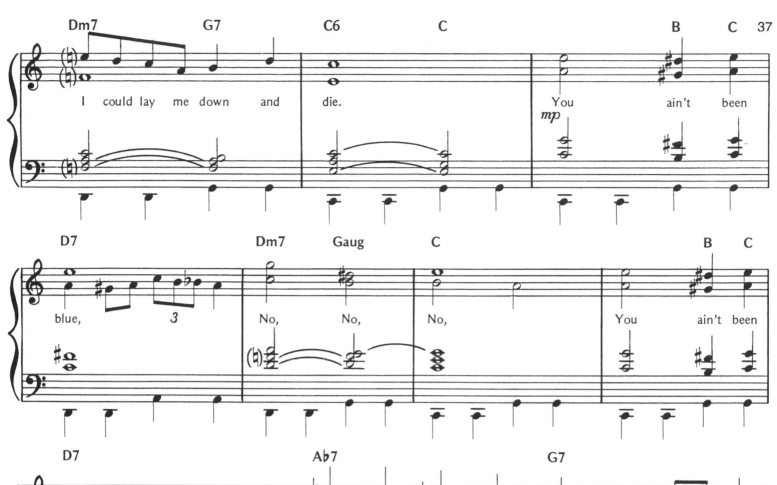

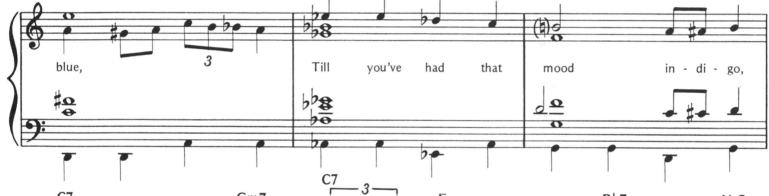

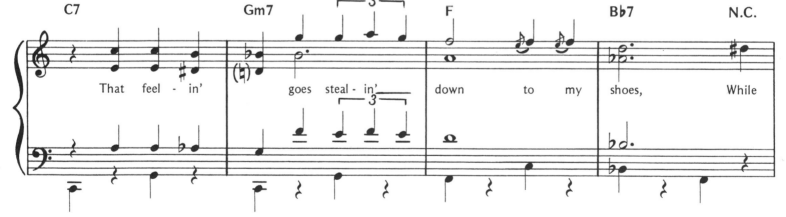

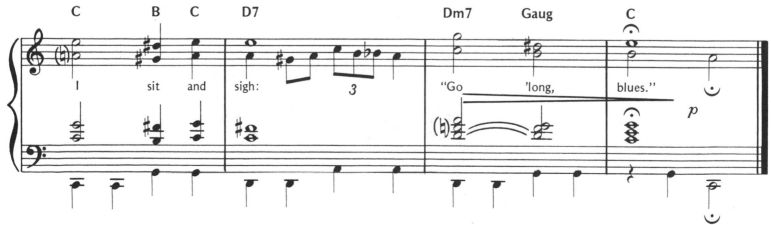

Moonglow

Electronic Organs
Upper: Flutes (or Tibias) 16', 8',
　　　　5⅓', 4', 2'
Lower: Flute 8', 4'
　　　　Diapason 8', Reed 8'
Pedal: 16', 8'
Vib./Trem: On, Fast

Tonebar Organs
Upper　86 6606 000
Lower: (00) 7732 211
Pedal:　55
Vib./Trem.: On, Fast

Words and Music by Will Hudson,
Eddie De Lange and Irving Mills

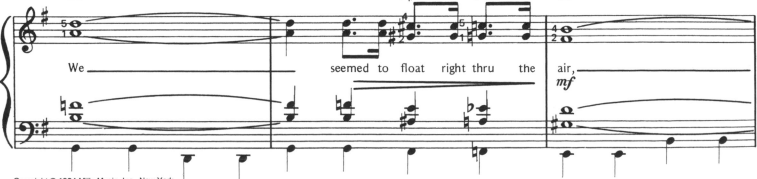

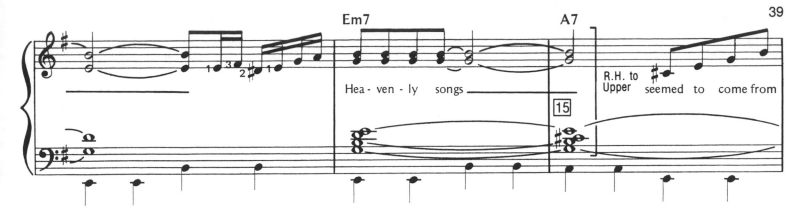

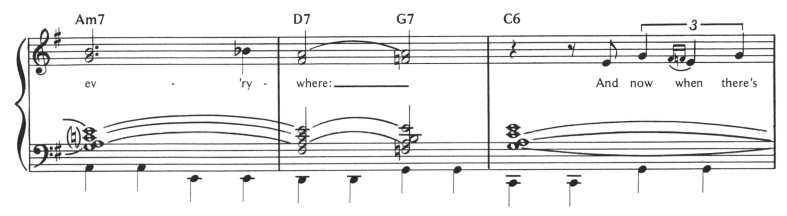

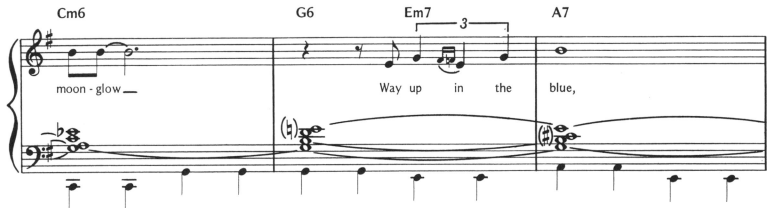

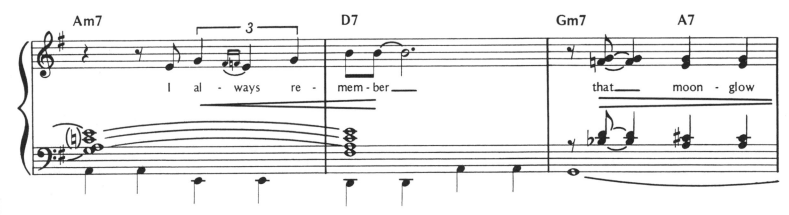

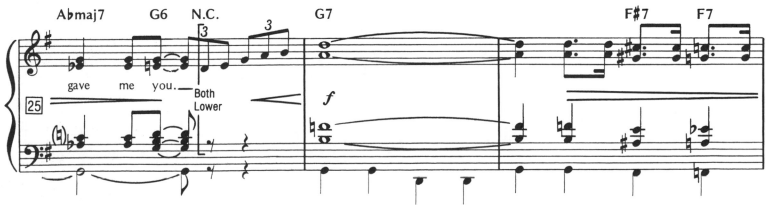

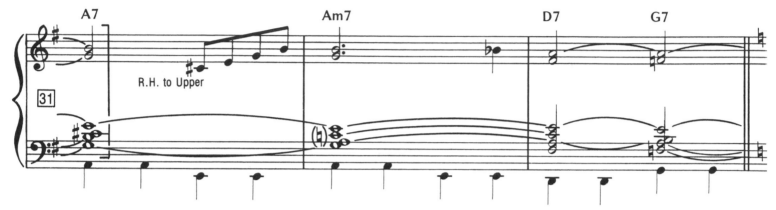

Old Devil Moon

from FINIAN'S RAINBOW

Words by E.Y. Harburg
Music by Burton Lane

DRAWBAR ORGANS

UPPER:	00 7654 000
LOWER:	(00) 5544 000(0)
PEDAL:	5-4
VIB/CHO:	On V-3

ALL OTHER ORGANS

UPPER:	Trumpet, Clarinet 8'
	Flute (Tibia) 8', 4'
LOWER:	Flute, String 8'
PEDAL:	Bourdon 16'
VIB:	On, Normal

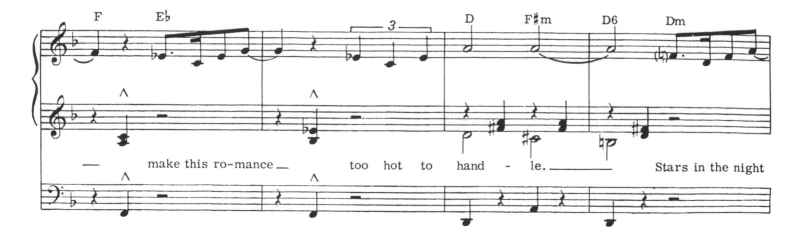

make this ro-mance ___ too hot to hand - le. ___ Stars in the night

___ blaz-ing their light ___ Can't hold a can - dle ___ to your raz - zle daz - zle.

You've got me fly - in' high and wide On a mag-ic car-pet

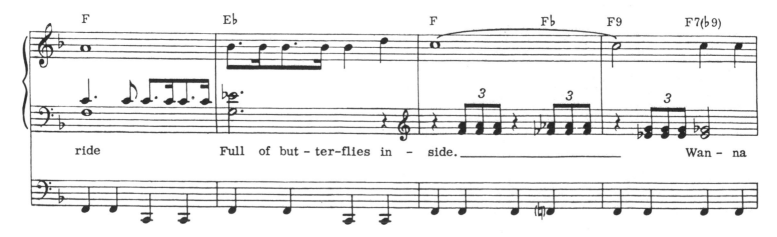

ride Full of but - ter-flies in - side. ___ Wan - na

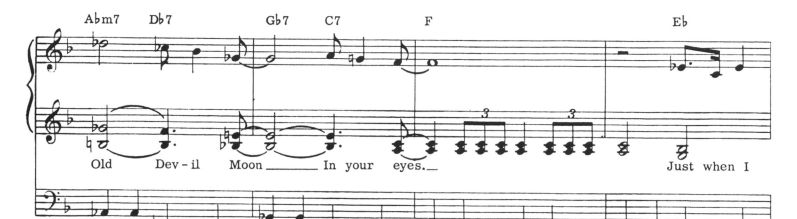

The Most Beautiful Girl in the World

from JUMBO

Electronic Organs
Upper: Flutes (or Tibias) 16', 8', 4', 2'
Lower: Flutes 8', 4', Diapason 8'
Pedal: String Bass
Vib./Trem.: On, Fast

Tonebar Organs
Upper: 52 5325 004
Lower: (00) 7345 312
Pedal: String Bass
Vib./Trem.: On, Fast

Words by Lorenz Hart
Music by Richard Rodgers

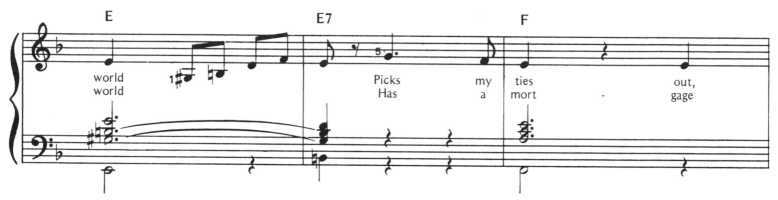

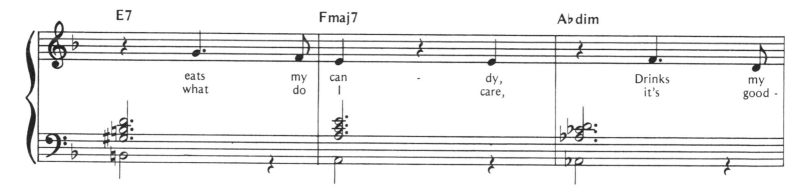

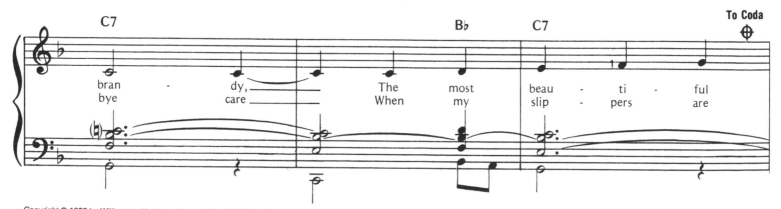

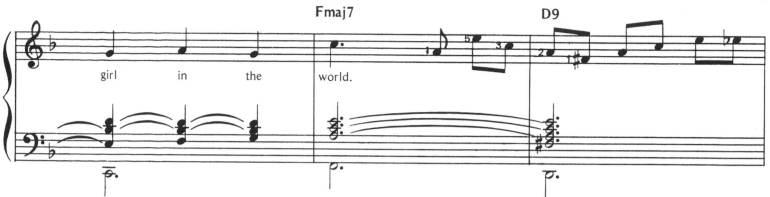

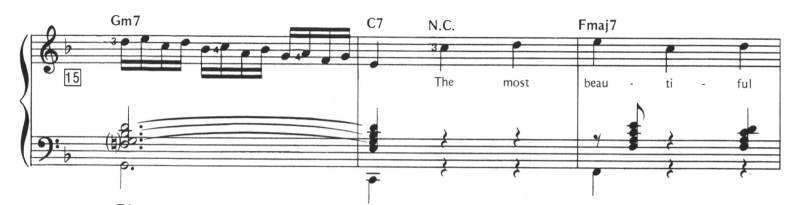

make me be - lieve it's a beau - ti - ful

world.

So - cial? Not a bit!

Nat - 'ral kind of wit,

She'd shine an - y - where,

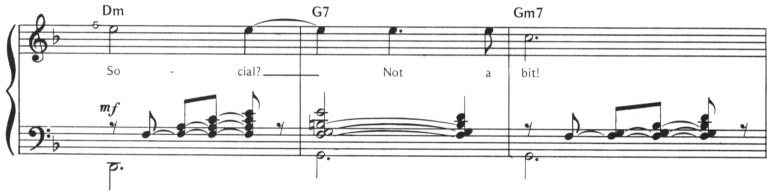

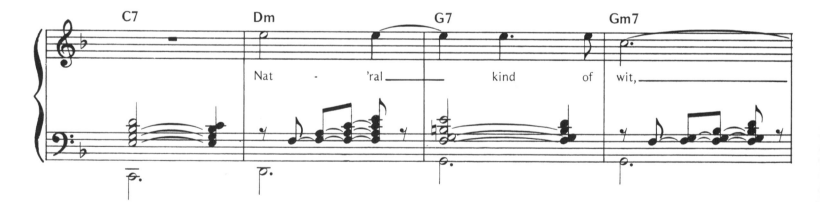

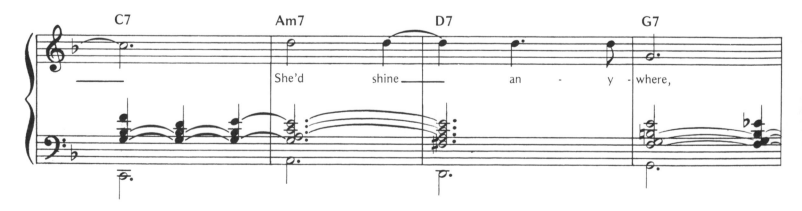

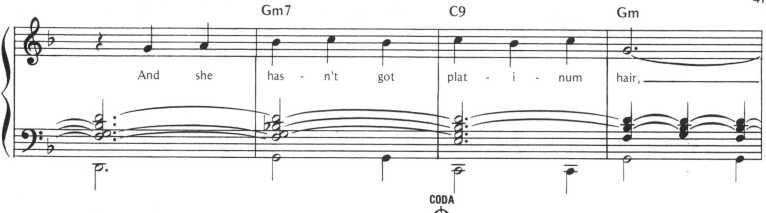

And she has- n't got plat- i- num hair, _____

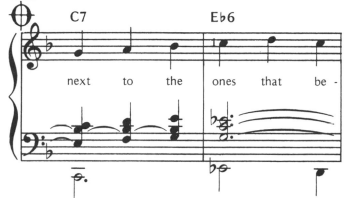

_____ The most

next to the ones that be -

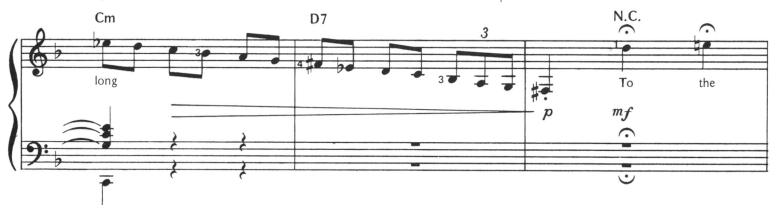

long

To the

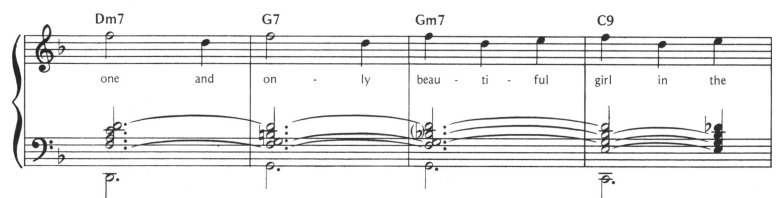

one and on - ly beau - ti - ful girl in the

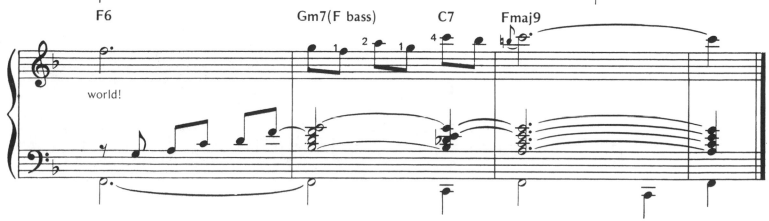

world!

On a Slow Boat to China

Electronic Organs
Upper: Flutes (or Tibias) 16', 8', 4', 2', 1'
Lower: Diapason 8'
       Flute 8', 4'
Pedal: Flute 16'
       String 8'
Vib./Trem.: On, Fast

Drawbar Organs
Upper: 80 7806 004
Lower: (00) 7503 000
Pedal: 46, Sustain
Vib./Trem.: On, Fast

By Frank Loesser

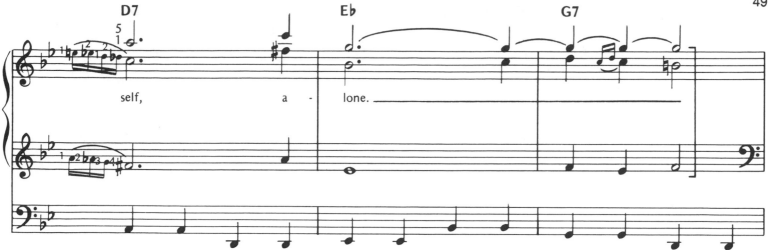

On the Sunny Side of the Street

Electronic Organs
Upper: Flutes (or Tibias) 16', 8', 5 1/3'
Lower: Flulte 8', String 8'
Pedal: 8' Sustain
Vib/Trem: On - Full

Drawbar Organs
Upper: 88 8060 000 (00)
Lower: (00) 6535 222 (0)
Pedal: 4 (0) 3 (0) (Spinet 5)
String Bass
Vib/Trem: On- Full

Lyric by Dorothy Fields
Music by Jimmy McHugh

*Spinet Organs — play L. H. on lower.

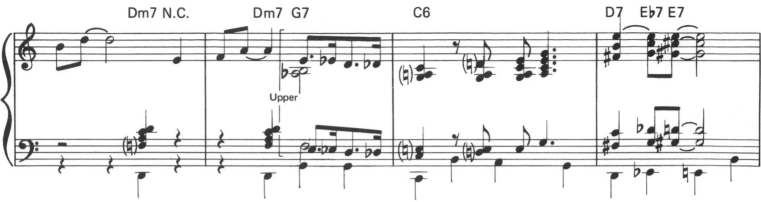

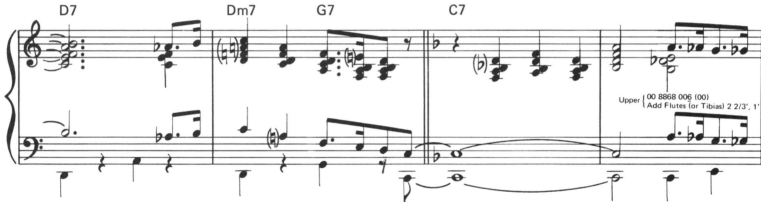

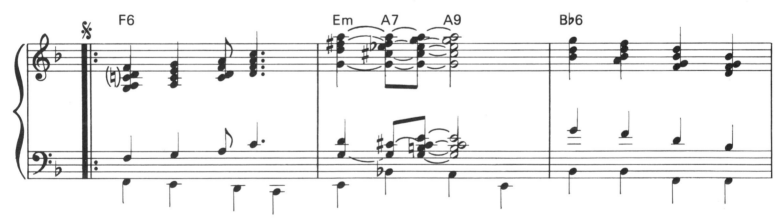

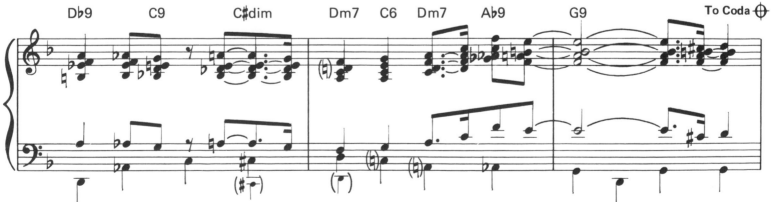

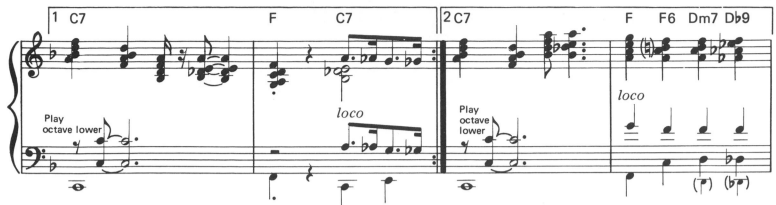

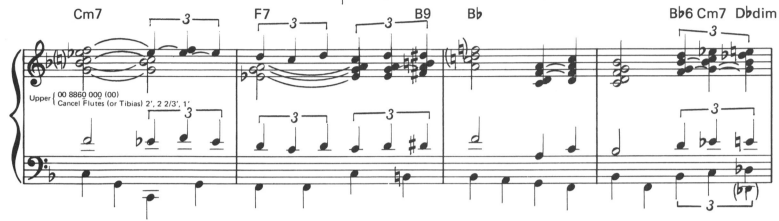

*Optional — left hand part may be played in octaves —
   one octave lower than written, if possible.

Paper Doll

Electronic Organs
Upper: Piano Preset or Flutes (or Tibias) 16′, 8′
Lower: Flute 8′, Diapason 8′
Pedal: 16′, String Bass
Vib./Trem.: Lower On, Fast
    (or Off)

Tonebar Organs
Upper: Piano Preset or 00 8400 000, Sustain
Lower: (00) 4311 000
Pedal: 34
Vib./Trem.: Lower On, Fast

Words and Music by
Johnny S. Black

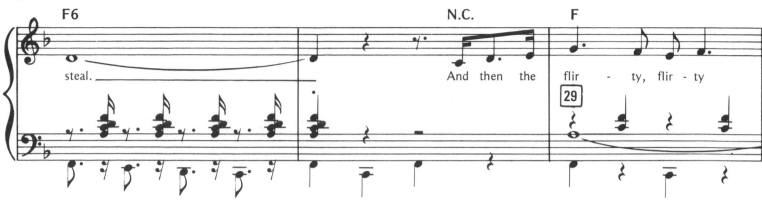

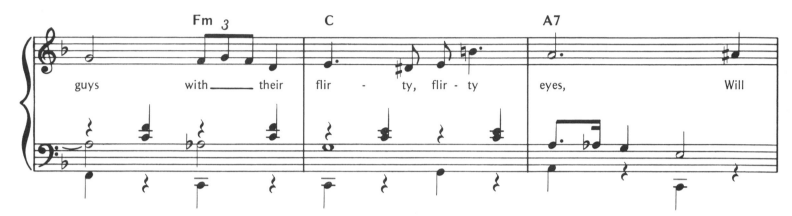

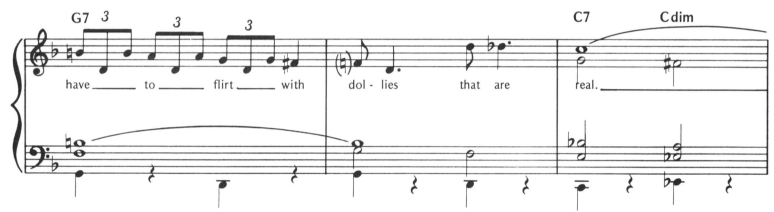

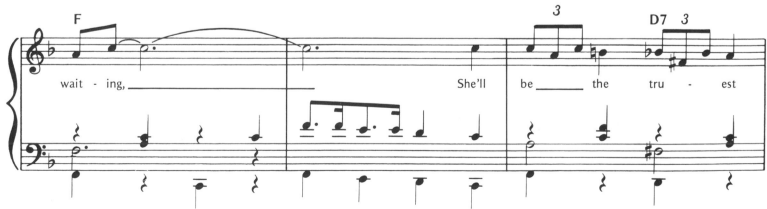

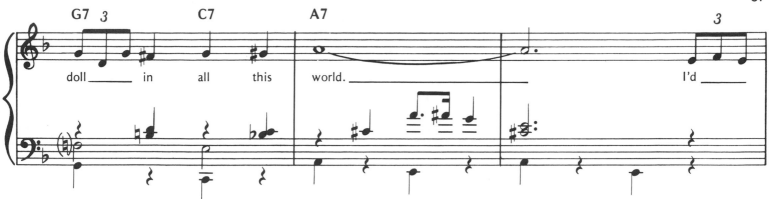

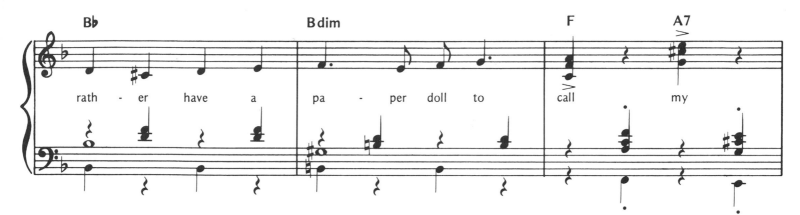

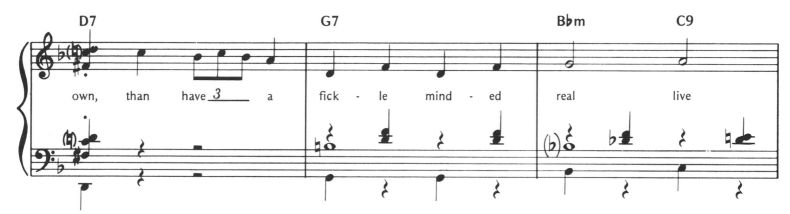

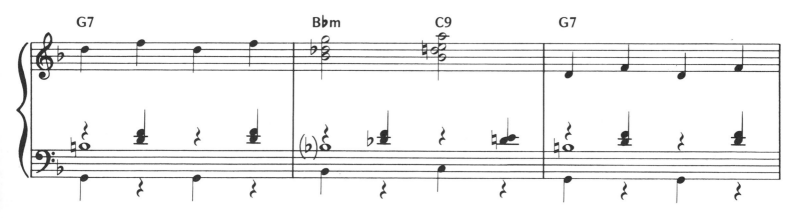

Route 66

Electronic Organs

Upper: Flutes (or Tibias) 16', 4', 2'
       String 8'
Lower: Diapason 8', Flute 8', String 4'
Pedal: 16', 8', Sustain
Vib./Trem.: Upper: Off
           Lower: On

Drawbar Organs

Upper: 60 0800 806
Lower: (00) 7654 432
Pedal: 48, Sustain
Vib./Trem.: Upper: Off (Opt.)
             Lower: On

By Bobby Troup

Moderately with a beat

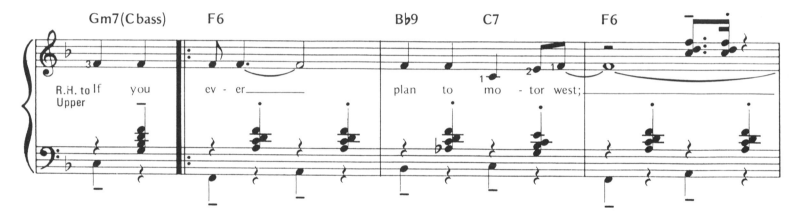

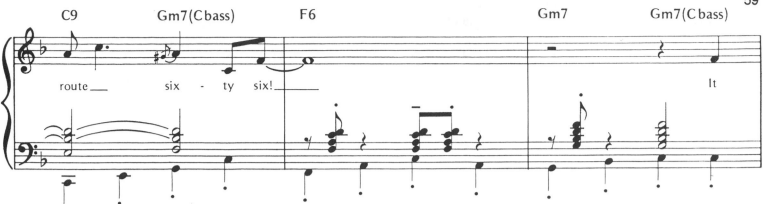

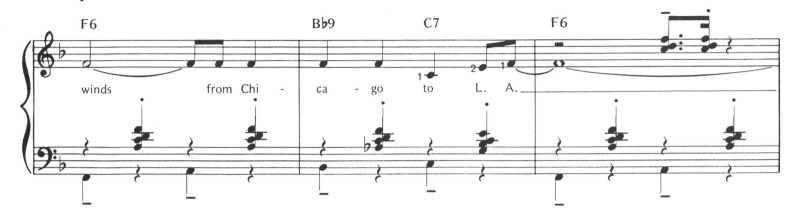

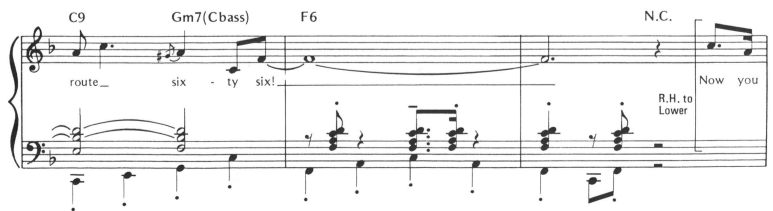

go thru Saint Loo-ey. Jop-lin, Mis-sour-i and Ok-la-hom-a Cit-y is might-

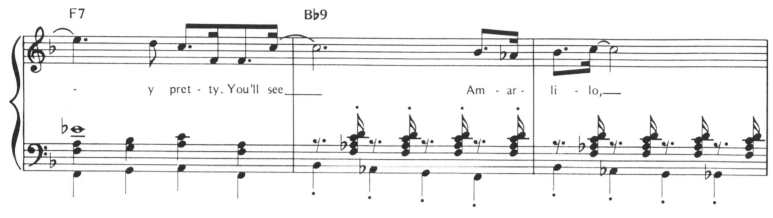

-y pret-ty. You'll see Am-ar-il-lo,

Gal-lup, New Mex-i-co; Flag-staff, Ar-i-zon-a;

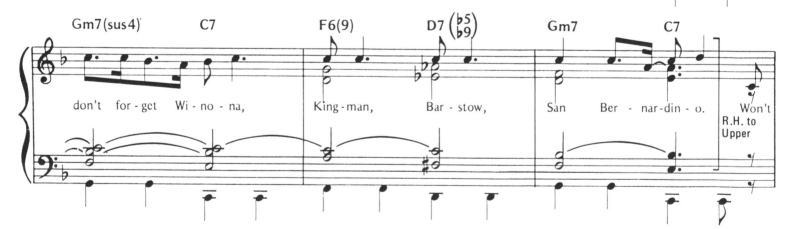

don't for-get Wi-no-na, King-man, Bar-stow, San Ber-nar-din-o. Won't
R.H. to
Upper

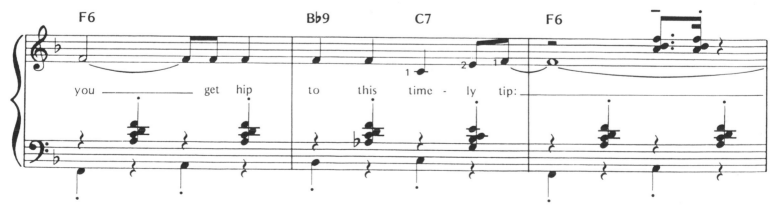

you get hip to this time-ly tip:

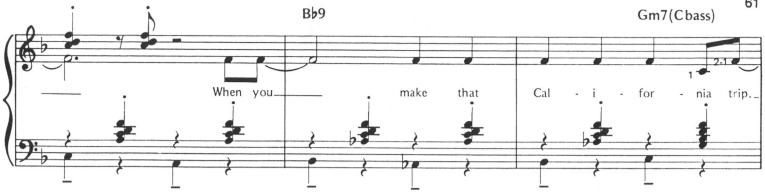

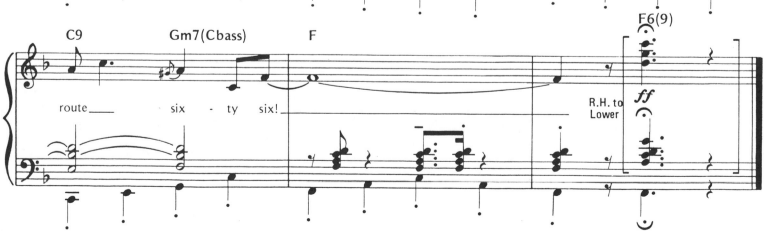

Sentimental Journey

Electronic Organs
Upper: Flutes (or Tibias) 16′, 5⅓′, 4′
Lower: Flute 8′, Diapason 8′
Pedal: String Bass
Vib./Trem.: On, Slow

Drawbar Organs
Upper: 84 0800 000
Lower: (00) 5303 000
Pedal: String Bass
Vib./Trem.: On, Slow

Words and Music by Bud Green,
Les Brown and Ben Homer

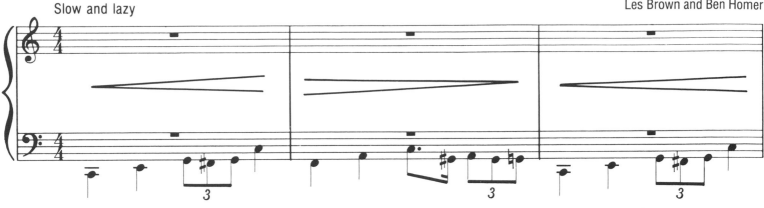

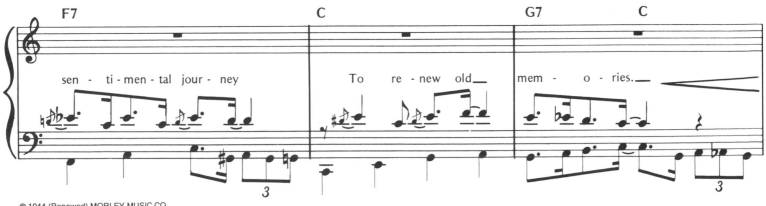

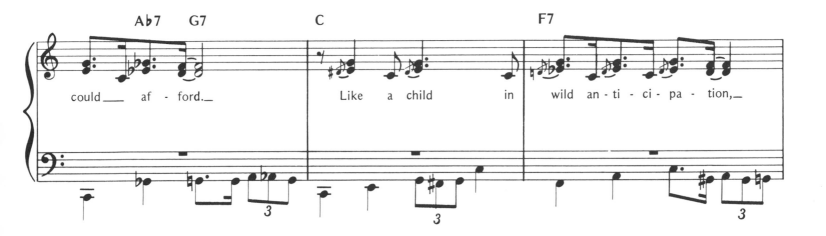

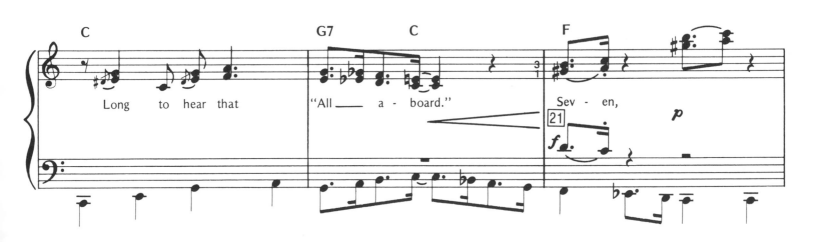

64

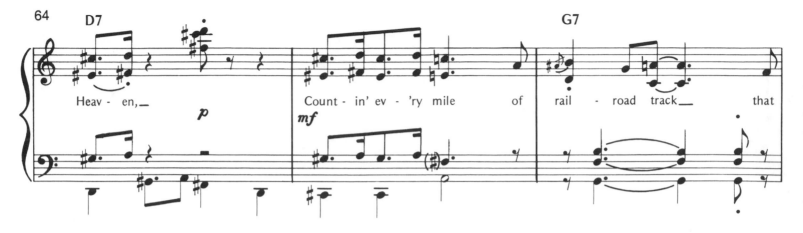

Heav - en,___ Count - in' ev - 'ry mile of rail - road track___ that

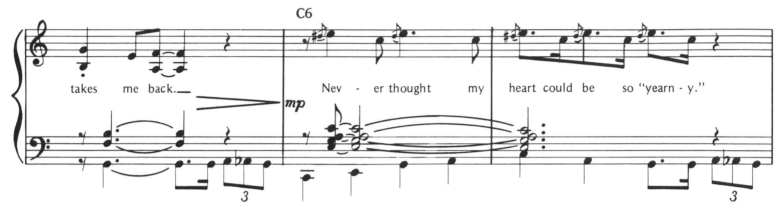

takes me back.___ Nev - er thought my heart could be so "yearn - y."

Why did I de - cide___ to roam?___ Got - ta take this

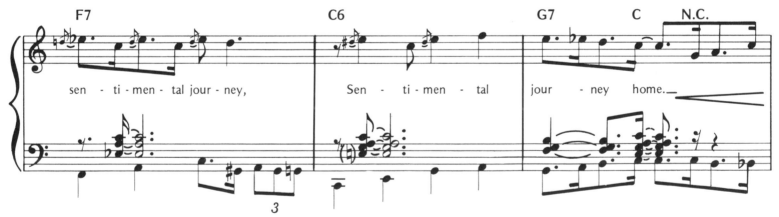

sen - ti - men - tal jour - ney, Sen - ti - men - tal jour - ney home.___

Stormy Weather

(Keeps Rainin' All the Time)
from COTTON CLUB PARADE OF 1933

Electronic Organs
Upper: Flutes (or Tibias) 16', 2'
    Add Percuss
Lower: Flutes 8', 4'
Pedal: 16'
Vib./Trem.: On, Slow
Rhythm: Swing or Fox Trot

Tonebar Organs
Upper: 80 0400 304
    Add Perc
Lower: (00) 7404 203
Pedal: 53
Vib./Trem.: On, Slow
Rhythm: Swing or Fox Trot

Lyric by Ted Koehler
Music by Harold Arlen

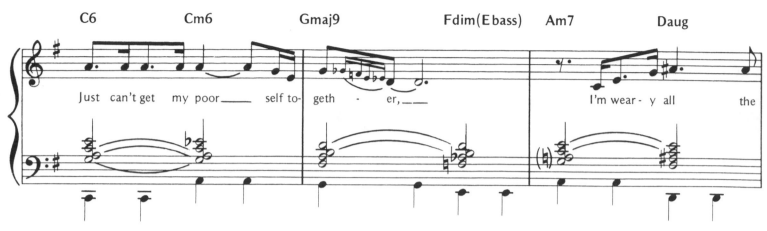

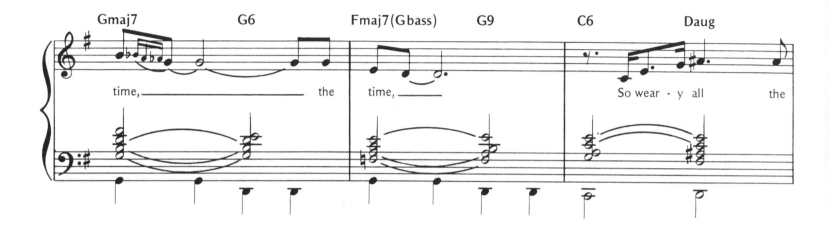

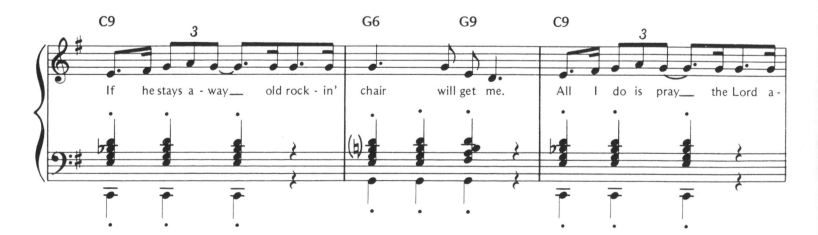

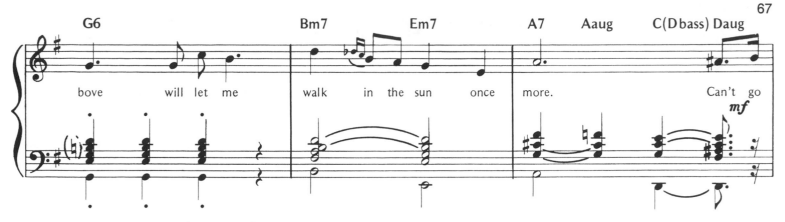

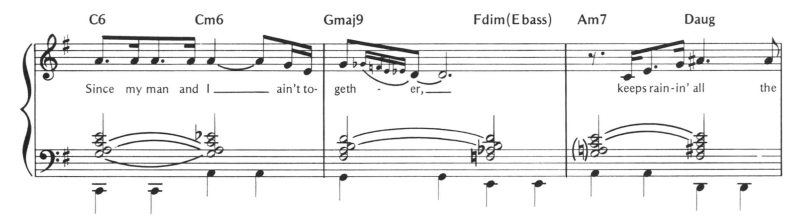

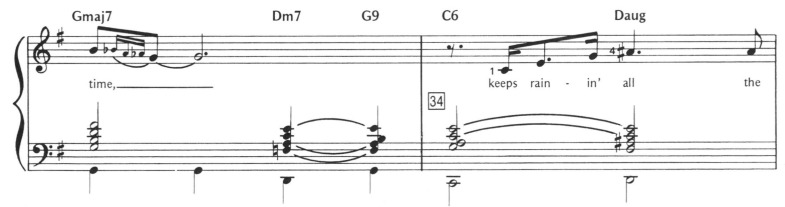

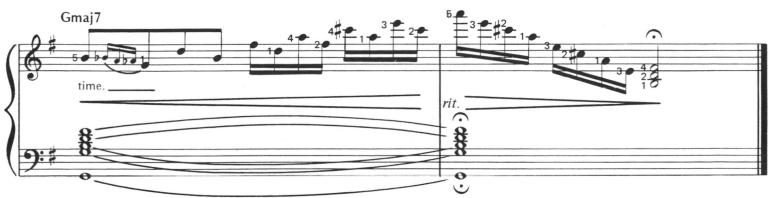

Sweet and Lovely

Electronic Organs
Upper: Flutes (or Tibias) 16', 4'
Lower: Flute 8', Diapason 8'
Pedal: 8'
Vib./Trem.: On, Fast

Tonebar Organs
Upper: 80 0800 000
Lower: (00) 5303 000
Pedal: 24
Vib./Trem.: Vibrato On

Words and Music by Gus Arnheim,
Charles N. Daniels and Harry Tobias

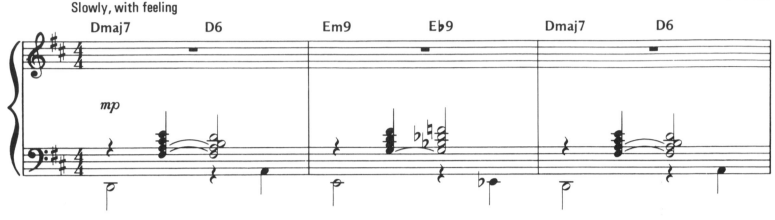

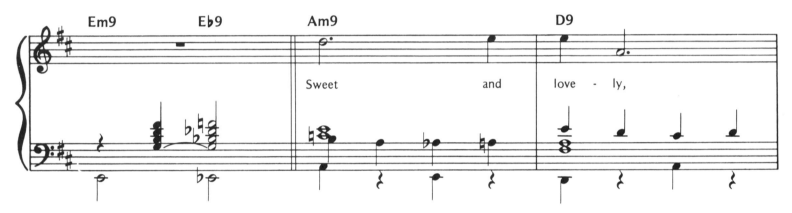

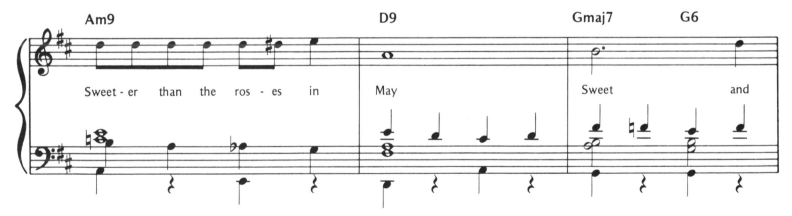

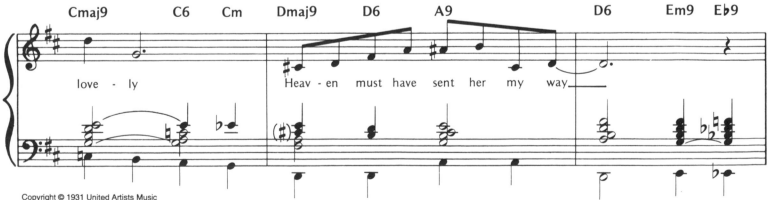

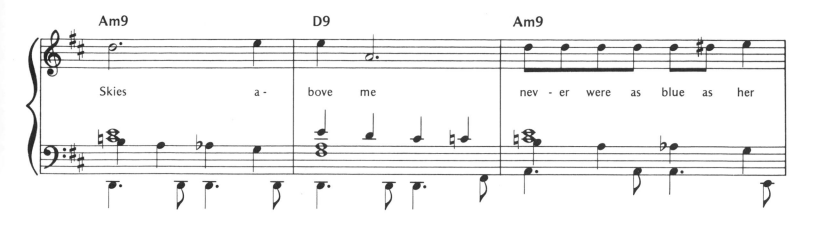

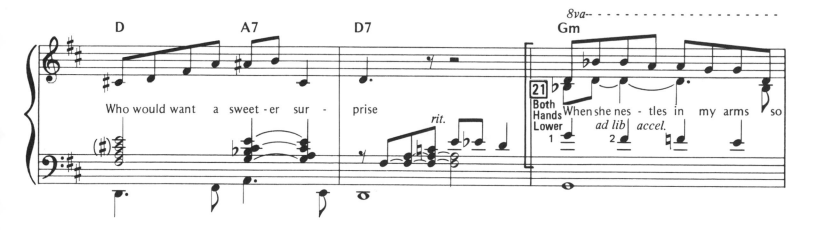

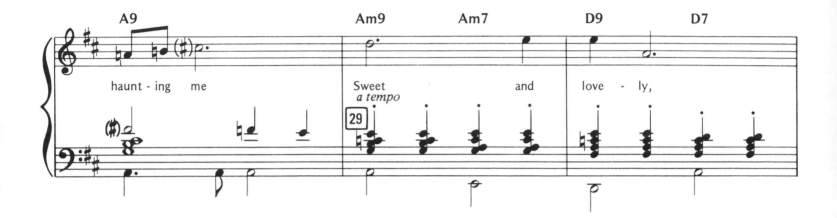

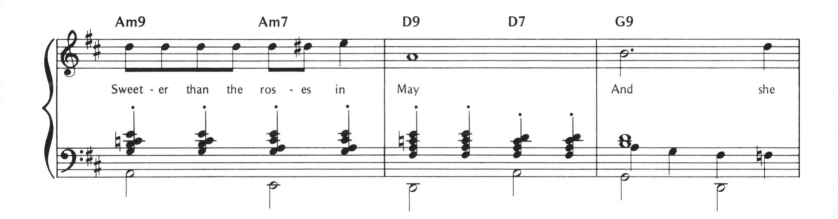

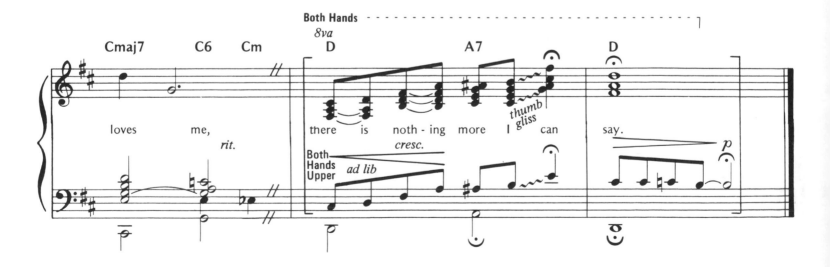

Witchcraft

Electronic Organs
Upper: Flutes (or Tibias) 8', 2'
      Diapason 8', String 8'
Lower: Flutes 8', 4'
Pedal: 16', 8'
Vib./Trem.: On, Fast

Drawbar Organs
Upper: 84 3456 780
Lower: (00) 8885 008
Pedal: 53
Vib./Trem.: On, Fast

Lyric by Carolyn Leigh
Music by Cy Coleman

Moderato (Slow 2)
8va to end

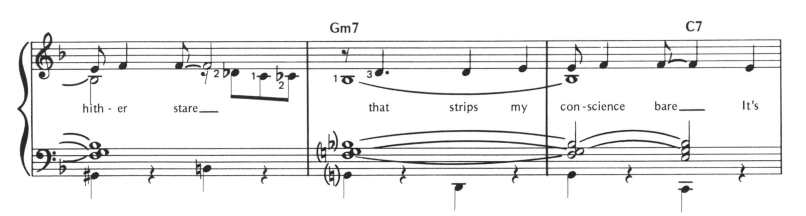

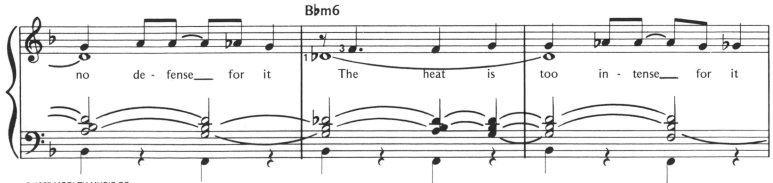

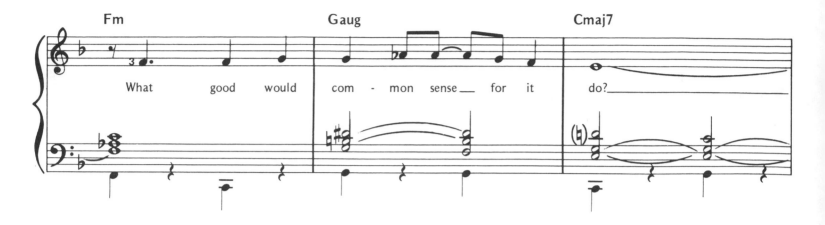

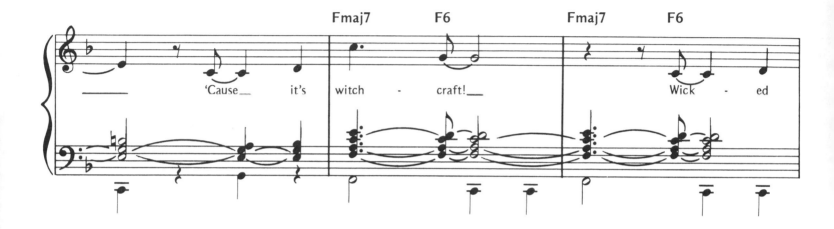

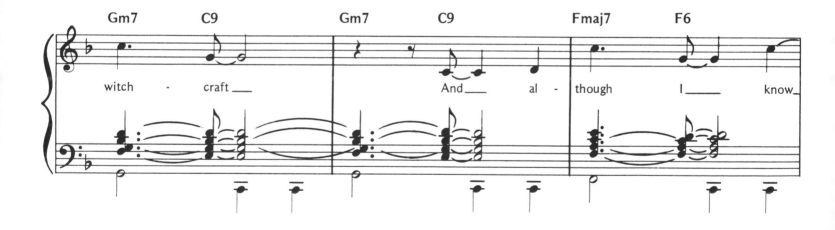

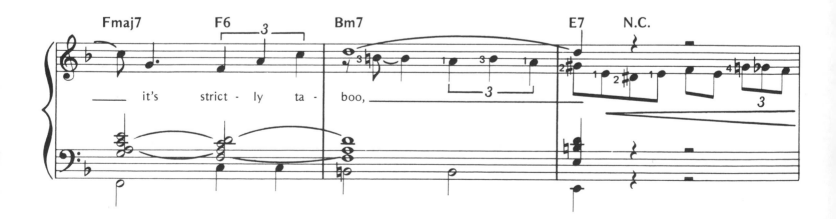

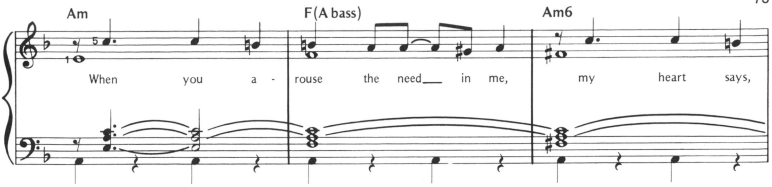

When you a-rouse the need___ in me, my heart says,

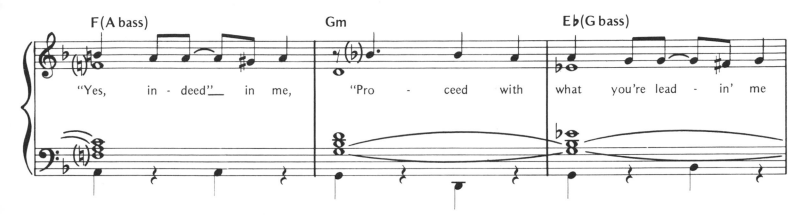

"Yes, in - deed"___ in me, "Pro - ceed with what you're lead - in' me

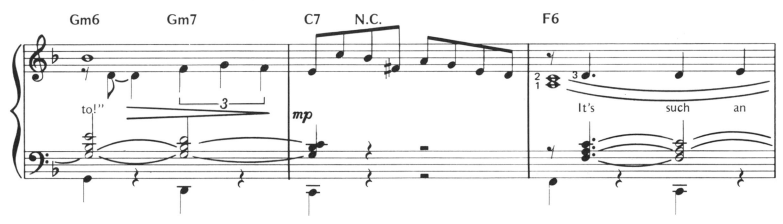

to!" It's such an

an - cient pitch___ But one I would-n't switch___

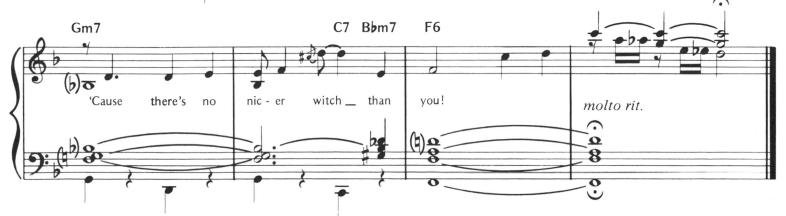

'Cause there's no nic - er witch___ than you!

molto rit.

Tenderly

from TORCH SONG

Electronic Organs
Upper: Flutes (or Tibias) 16', 8', 4'
Lower: Melodia 8', Reed 8'
Pedal: String Bass
Vib./Trem.: On, Fast

Drawbar Organs
Upper: 80 4800 000
Lower: (00) 7334 011
Pedal: String Bass
Vib./Trem.: On, Fast

Lyric by Jack Lawrence
Music by Walter Gross

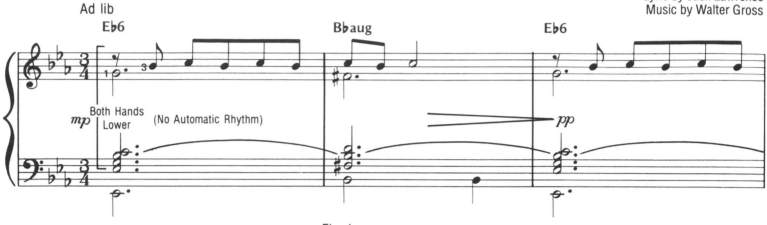

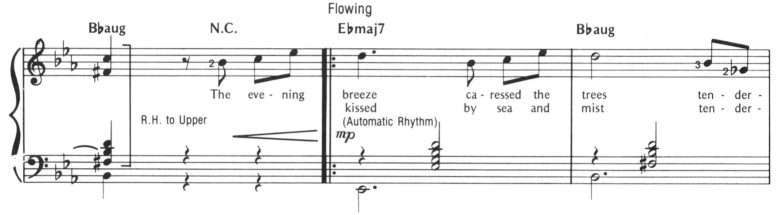

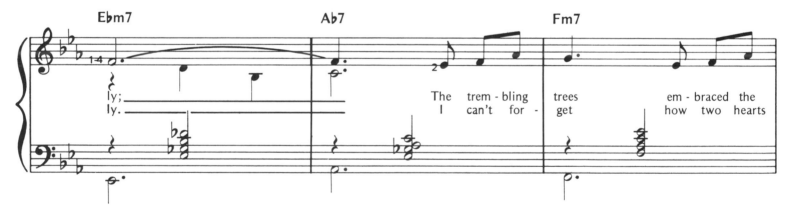

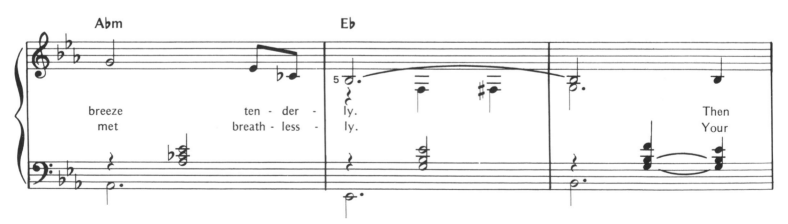

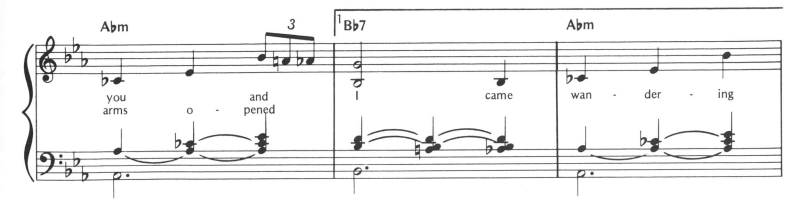

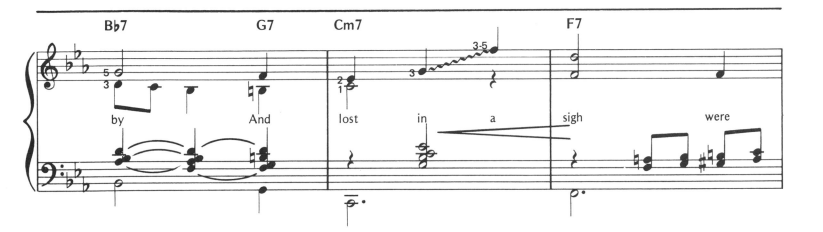

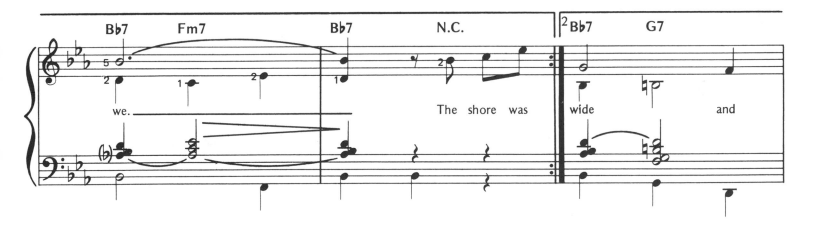

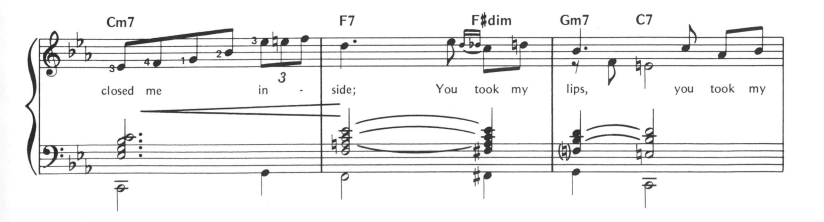

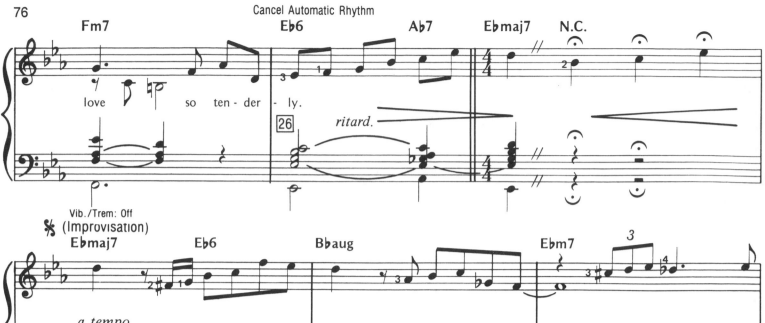

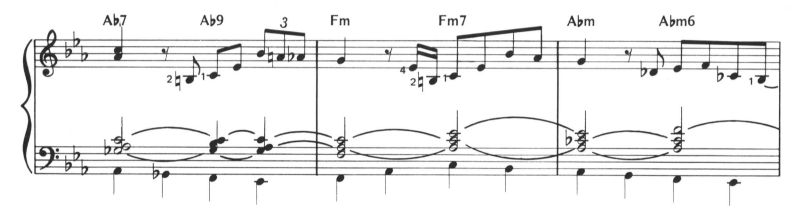

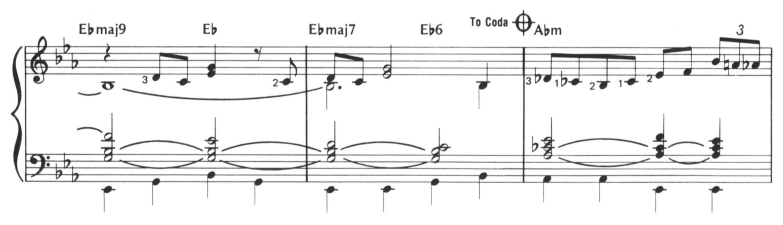

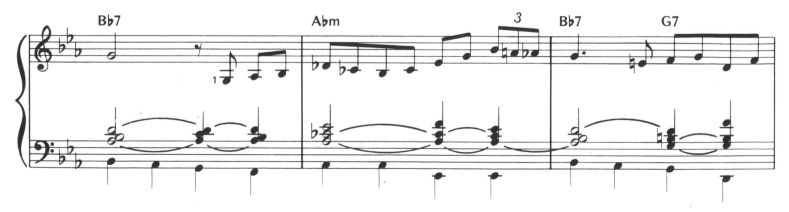

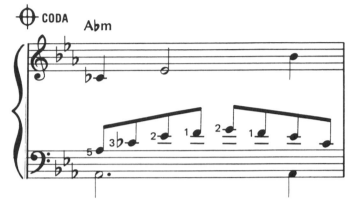

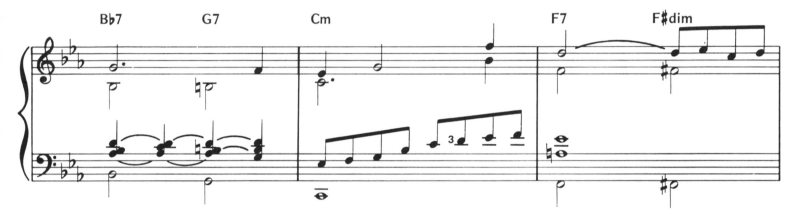

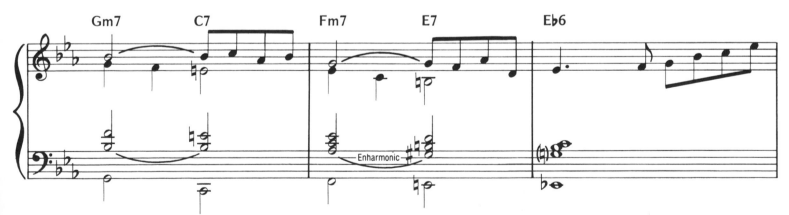

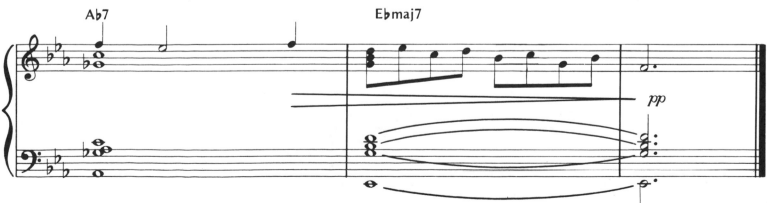

You'd Be So Nice to Come Home To

from SOMETHING TO SHOUT ABOUT

Electronic Organs

Upper: Flutes (or Tibias) 16′, 8′,
 5⅓′, 2⅔′, 2′
Lower: Flutes 8′, 4′, String 8′
Pedal: 8′, Sustain
Vib./Trem.: Off

Tonebar. Organs

Upper: 86 5434 568
Lower: (00) 6503 406
Pedal: 44 String Bass
Vib./Trem.: Off

Words and Music by
Cole Porter

Slow Beguine

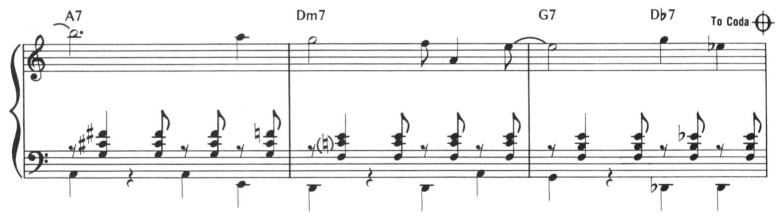

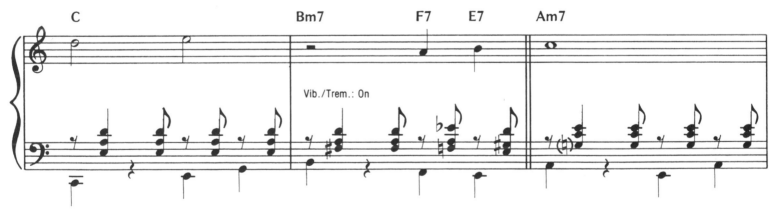

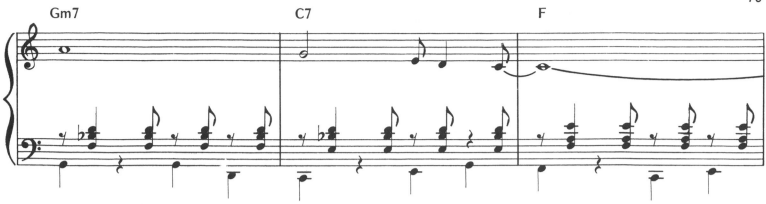

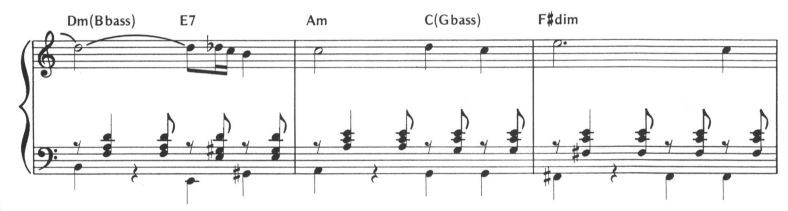

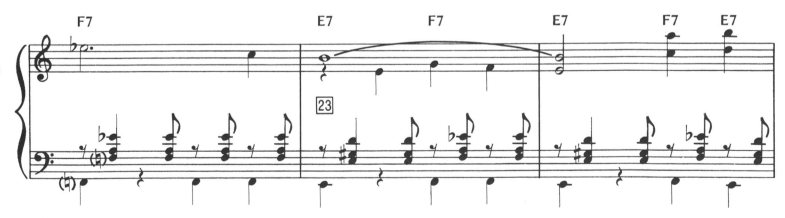

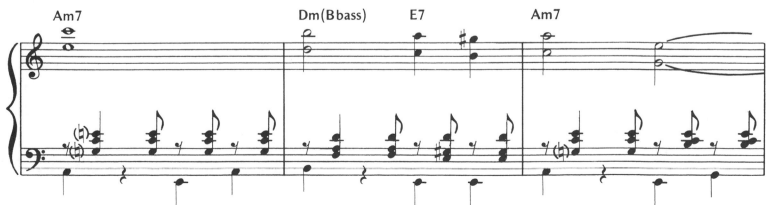

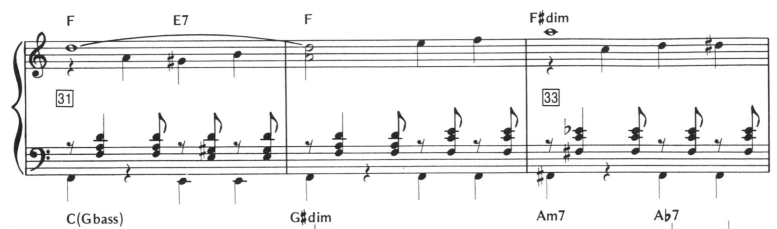

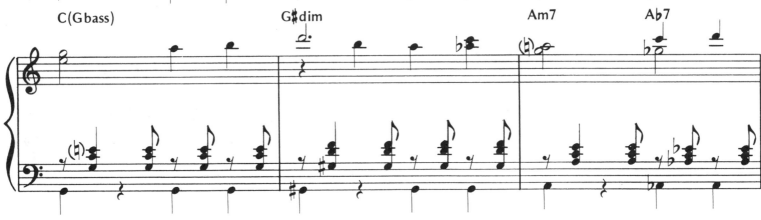

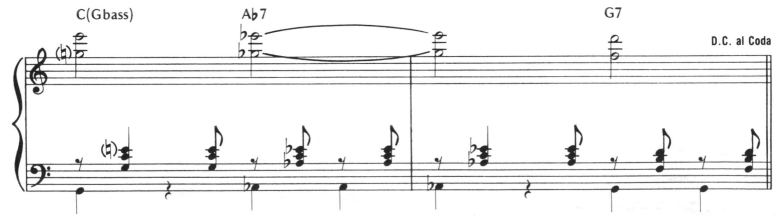

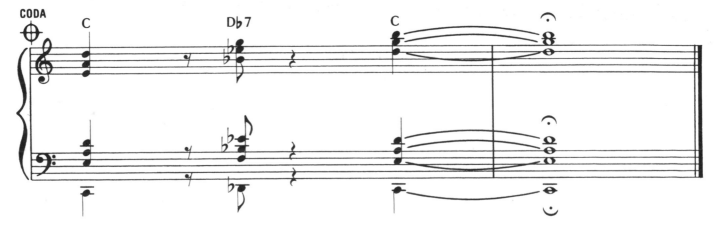